Letts go to
Denmark

by Harold Dennis-Jones

KW-763-902

First published 1975
by Charles Letts and Company Limited
Diary House, Borough Road, London SE1 1DW

Designed by Ed Perera

Cover: Vallø Castle, photograph: Danish Tourist Board

Photographs: Danish Tourist Board, pp 27, 30, 32, 33, 35, 41, 46, 49, 52
National Travel Association of Denmark, pp 20, 37, 65
Harold Dennis-Jones, pp 39, 45
Illustration: Ed Perera

© Text: Harold Dennis-Jones

Standard Book Number 85097 119 5

Printed in Great Britain by
McFarlane & Erskine Limited, Dalkeith

Letts Holiday Guides

Contents

Facts at your Fingertips

Passports and Visas

To travel to Denmark you need either a valid full passport (blue cover) or a valid British Visitor's Passport (pink). The former is valid worldwide for 10 years and costs £5. The latter can be used only for Denmark and certain West European countries (including those you are likely to travel through on surface routes to Denmark): it lasts 1 year and costs £1.50.

To get a full passport you must apply to the right Passport Office for the address where you live: this, together with all other requirements, is clearly shown on the application forms which you can obtain from any Passport Office or Principal Post Office (listed in your local phone directory) and from most travel agents. British Visitors' Passports are obtained over the counter by personal application at any Principal Post Office: apart from 2 passport-sized photographs, reasonable proof of identity is required (eg, medical card, birth certificate, or out-of-date passport). A wife (but not husband) and children under 16 can be included on either type of passport. Over 16s require their own travel documents. Unlike most countries however Denmark does not recognise a passport as valid unless all the people entered on it are present.

You show your passport at the frontier only when you enter the first Scandinavian country on your itinerary and again when you finally leave Scandinavia. Visas for stays of up to 3 months are not needed by citizens of the UK, USA, and most Commonwealth countries—but this time limit has to cover your entire continuous stay in Scandinavia.

Visitors must register with the police within 24 hours of arrival. Remember, if you stay with friends or in a rented chalet, for instance—you must do it yourself.

Insurance

UK residents visiting Denmark can obtain medical attention on exactly the same terms as Danish residents. Very little is completely free but charges are low: for even a major operation you pay only a few pounds. Additional insurance to cover possible costs of extra hotel accommodation, special flights home and so on is highly advisable. It costs very little and can be obtained through Lloyd's, Europ Assistance, and many other insurance companies (see addresses on p 18). 'Holiday travel' policies cover you also against loss of deposits if you have to cancel at the last moment, and can often be arranged by the travel firm you book with. The motoring organisations, the Caravan Club, and other organisations include

3

personal insurance along with the extra cover needed for cars and caravans (addresses see p 18).

Customs

Coming from the UK you may take into Denmark everything intended for bona fide personal use, including jewellery, cameras, musical instruments, portable radio and typewriter, and sports equipment including boats (whether entering by sea or by road).

Duty-free allowances have been standardised throughout the Common Market countries, which include both Britain and Denmark. A distinction is made between goods bought from ordinary shops in EEC countries (ie with local tax included) and those acquired from airport or ferry duty-free shops or non-EEC countries. To qualify for the larger allowance you must arrive direct from an EEC country. Different types of goods may be bought in different classes of shops, but if you buy, say, alcohol in both EEC and duty-free shops, the lower allowance applies.

Whether going to Denmark or returning to UK you can bring in the following items without paying duty (tobacco and alcohol allowances apply only if you are over 17):

EEC		Non-EEC
	Tobacco Goods	
300	Cigarettes	200 (tipped or untipped)
	or	
150	Cigarillos	100
	or	
75	Cigars	50
	or	
400g (about 15oz)	Tobacco	250g (about 8oz)
	Alcoholic Drinks	
1½ litres	over 38.8° proof	1 litre
(2 bottles)	(22° Gay-Lussac)	(1⅓ bottles)
	or	
3 litres	not over 38,8° proof or fortified or sparkling wine	2 litres
	plus	
3 litres	still table wine	2 litres
75g (3 fl oz)	**Perfume**	50g (2 fl oz)
⅜ litre	**Toilet Water**	¼ litre
£50 worth	**Other Goods**	£10 worth

Climate and Clothing

Denmark's climate is in general not very different from Britain's, except that winters are a little colder and summers mostly a little warmer. Spring comes suddenly and is sometimes warm as well as delightful to see. Summer, from June until early October, can produce bouts of wonderful clear, hot, sunny weather. Autumn brings a mass of colours, especially in the beech woods found in many parts of the country. Winters are rarely as mild as in Britain, but everything and everywhere is kept so warm—including theatres, station concourses, and public transport—that you need only heavy overcoats but not thick suits or dresses.

The clothes needed in Denmark are exactly the same as those required for holiday wear in UK. Formal clothes are not needed in recognised holiday resorts unless you are staying in top-grade hotels, when lounge suits and formal dresses are advisable for evenings.

Currency

No limits are placed on the amount of Danish or foreign currency and traveller's cheques that you may take into or out of Denmark. But you are not allowed to take more than £25 in banknotes out of Britain, and if you are carrying more than 2000 kroner when you leave Denmark you may be asked to prove that this sum was either imported into Denmark in Danish currency or acquired there by the sale of foreign currency.

The boats operating between Britain and Denmark have exchange offices on board, and the airport has an exchange office that is open continuously. There is, therefore, no real need to buy Danish currency before departure. Traveller's cheques are the easiest way of carrying your money.

Inside Denmark special exchange bureaux cater for visitors at all the main entry points, remaining open as long as passengers are entering or leaving the country. Special exchange offices can also be found in large towns and main tourist centres: those in central Copenhagen often remain open until 22.00 or 24.00. The larger hotels also have exchange counters. Elsewhere you can change your money and traveller's cheques in banks which are open mostly between 09.30 and 15.00 on Monday to Friday, but closed on Saturdays. In provincial towns some banks close for lunch between 12.00 and 14.00 but stay open longer in the afternoon. Some banks open also on Thursday and Friday afternoons from 16.00 to 18.00

Denmark's currency unit is the krone ('crown': plural *kroner*), abbreviated kr, divided into 100 øre (singular *øre*), 5, 10, and 25 øre. Coins of 1 and 5 kroner—all of silver-nickel—and 10, 50, 100 and 500 kroner banknotes are in general circulation. At the time of writing the exchange rate is roughly £1 = 15 kr. While considerable fluctuations are possible the following exchange equivalents will act as a rough guide:

Krone—£ equivalents at 15 kr = £1

kr	1	2	3	5	10	25	50	100
£p	7p	12p	20p	33p	67p	£1.67	£3.33	£6.66

£—Krone equivalents at £1 = 15 kr

£p	1p	2p	3p	5p	10p	50p	£1	£5
kr	0.15	0.30	0.45	0.75	1.50	7.50	15.00	75.00

Time

Denmark keeps Central European Time which is the same as British Time in summer but 1 hour behind in winter (from late October till mid-March).

Getting There

By Air

All international flights to Denmark operate to and from Kastrup Airport just outside Copenhagen. Starting-points in Britain are London-Heathrow and Manchester. The airlines concerned are British Airways, SAS Scandinavian Airlines, and Aer Lingus Irish Airlines. Prices from London in autumn 1974 were: tourist-class single £57.50, 1st-class £85.15, with a 'Cut Price' tourist-class return fare of £69.25 valid for 2 months. These 'Cut Price' tickets must be bought at least 2 months before departure, and the return journey can begin only 10 days after outward travel. No stopovers are permitted.

By Sea

The main ferry service between Harwich and Esbjerg is operated by DFDS (Det Forenede Dampskib Selskab—though the full title is no longer used outside Denmark). The same company operates between Newcastle and Esbjerg in summer. The journey time from Harwich is 18 hours and from Newcastle 19½. Passenger fares range from roughly £17-£41.50 according to cabin: cars cost £14 irrespective of length, with a surcharge of 50% if over 6 feet high. DFDS's ships have excellent facilities and service: meals are extra and are paid for on the vessel.

A slower and more unusual, but still thoroughly comfortable, way of reaching Copenhagen is aboard the Russian vessels of the Baltic Steamship Company. The journey from London to Copenhagen takes a little over 2 days and costs £15-£56 according to cabin.

including meals. Sailings never exceed 6 per month. Cars are not carried.

It is also possible to sail from London or Immingham to Gothenburg (Göteborg) in Sweden by Swedish Lloyd or Tor Line and also from Harwich to Bremerhaven or Hamburg in West Germany and continue to Denmark by train and boat. Motorists have an even wider choice of routes, all covered by a single fixed-price ticket (see p 21).

By Rail and Sea
Special trains connect London (daily) and Manchester (not Sundays) with DFDS sailings from Harwich. At Esbjerg Harbour another special train called *Englænderen* (The Englishman) takes passengers to Copenhagen, with stops at major points along the route enabling them to reach other destinations throughout Denmark. A London-Copenhagen 2nd-class single costs £28 and 1st-class £30 (return double).

There are also through rail-and-boat services via Ostend or Hook of Holland which cross into Denmark either at the South Jutland town of Padborg or make direct for Copenhagen via the short Puttgarden-Rødbyhavn ferry. Journeys on these routes take roughly 24 hours and cost £28-£30 2nd-class single (£32-£35 1st-class) with return fares slightly less than double.

Internal Transport

Airlines Kastrup Airport (Copenhagen) has regular connections to 9 destinations in Jutland and also to Odense on Funen (Fyn) and Rønne on Bornholm. Single fares range from about 120 kr to around 230 kr, with sizeable reductions for families and groups, children and young people, and everyone over 65. If you fly to Copenhagen from Britain or countries further west, such as the USA, international fare regulations enable you to have free tickets between Copenhagen and destinations to the west—ie, not to Rønne, which lies east of the capital. It is, however, essential to ask for the extra ticket when booking your flight to Denmark. SAS and travel agents holding IATA licences can give you full details.

Rail Danish State Railways (DSB), helped by a few private railways on outlying lines, maintain an efficient rail network throughout Denmark. Where necessary, services are supplemented by ferries and buses, many of them owned by DSB. Basic fare levels are roughly similar to Britain's, though many reductions are available (see below). Trains are comfortable, very efficiently run, and extremely well heated in winter. Since distances are relatively short, dining cars are not provided—though snacks and drinks can always be bought from mobile trolleys on all major trains. Longer-distance journeys always involve transferring to a ferry at some point—in some cases the whole train goes aboard, saving you the trouble of changing. This provides the opportunity for a meal—avidly seized by most Danes, so that it is as well to be prepared for an unashamed scramble as soon as the train slows for the ferry.

Couchette sleeping accommodation is provided only on night expresses between Copenhagen, Funen, and Jutland. Children are well cared for. Main-line trains all have compartments (labelled *børnkupé*) reserved for mothers with children under 4, main stations similarly have rooms where mothers can change nappies, warm bottles, and so on, and on the longer ferries between Zeeland and Jutland games rooms are available for older children. Children under 4 not occupying a seat travel free: those between 4 and 12 pay half price.

Numerous other reduced-rate fares are available (details from the Danish Tourist Office; address p 18).

Coach The only long-distance coach services in Denmark are those which make use of the direct ferry routes on the Copenhagen-North Jutland runs. Extensive networks of local services however radiate from all main and many minor towns. Central bus stations are usually at or very close to railway stations, and timetables are arranged so that train-bus connections are easy. Through tickets, covering also the journey's bus sections, can be bought at railway stations. Where buses and trains cover the same route tickets can be used on either. Except in a few rare cases road travel tickets can be bought also on the buses. Fares are the same as for 2nd-class rail travel.

Inside towns you pay fixed rates for journeys of whatever length. Inside Copenhagen you pay 1.50 kr for a ticket entitling you to travel on whatever buses you like inside 1 hour. A book *(polet)* of 8 tickets can be bought for 10.00 kr. Combined 1-hour tickets covering both bus and S-train travel cost 1.80 kr. A route map *(Liniekort),* obtainable free from the town's Tourist Information Office, travel agents, and elsewhere, is essential if you intend to do much travelling by public transport in the capital.

Ferries Nearly 100 ferry services operate inside Danish waters. Only a very few are reserved for cyclists and pedestrians: the rest carry also cars and buses. A leaflet giving full details of all main services can be obtained free from the Danish National Tourist Office (see p 18). Unless included in the train or coach fare, ferry tickets can be bought either on the quayside or on board. Advance bookings are not necessary for passengers without vehicles, or with only cycles or motorcycles, but are essential in summer for cars. Places on ferries operated by Danish State Railways can be booked at any railway station: on other routes reservations can be made by phone at the numbers shown in the National Tourist Office's list. Nearly all ferries have bars and buffets, and restaurants are available on the longer routes.

Taxis Taxis are readily available throughout Denmark and most drivers speak at least adequate English. Those that are available for hire display a sign saying *FRI*, but it is usually easier to go to a taxi rank (eg, at the railway station) or to telephone (you can use English). In Copenhagen the numbers are 35 35 35 and 35 14 20. All Copenhagen taxis are fitted with meters and these show the total price to be paid, including VAT (*MOMS* in Danish) and tip—in other cases give 15%. Prices are perhaps a little higher than Britain's —or seem so with everything included on the meter.

Car hire Anyone aged more than 20-25 who holds a full (not provisional) driving licence can hire a car without difficulty. Major international hire firms, such as Avis, Carop, Hertz, InterRent, and others, are represented in Denmark and there are many smaller local firms. Prices range around 43 kr per day or 260 kr per week for an Opel Kadett plus 0.57 kr per km: 745 kr per week with unlimited mileage. Certain firms hire also car-caravan outfits and motor caravans (campers). Motor scooters and mopeds are available in main towns and major tourist areas—provided you are over 21. Hirers' addresses can be obtained from the local Tourist Information Office.

Cycling Denmark is a cyclists' paradise, much appreciated by the Danes themselves. Special cycle tracks (marked *CYCLESTI*) are provided in picturesque parts of the country and also in towns such as Copenhagen where you can cycle to and from many suburbs almost without encountering other road traffic. Pre-booked cycling tours, which you can start on any day you wish, are organised by a number of provincial tourist offices, with accommodation in Youth Hostels (see p 11). Up-to-date information about these holidays can be obtained from the National Tourist Office. If you decide to tour Denmark by push-bike, note that cycles are carried free on country buses (not in towns) either on the roof or on special racks at the rear, and very cheaply on trains.

Cycles can be hired in most towns and tourist areas for about 10 kr per day, plus a deposit of about 25 kr (take your passport as proof of identity when hiring). Danish Railways hire bikes from a dozen-odd stations: other hire addresses can be obtained from local Tourist Information Offices, who will also advise on routes.

Accommodation

A full range of attractive accommodation is available in Denmark. It includes hotels of every sort, country inns, guesthouses, furnished holiday chalets, modern Youth Hostels, and first-rate campsites on which caravans are also accepted. Prices, especially in hotels, are relatively high. But you always get excellent value for your money. Summarised information about accommodation of every type is available free on request from the Danish National Tourist Office: if you need further details local Tourist Information Offices can always supply them, either in advance or after your arrival.

Hotels Denmark has no system of official hotel classification. Prices however are competitive, and provide a pretty accurate indication of each hotel's facilities and standard. Establishments can in general be divided into five main categories—luxury and 1st-class hotels; more modest 'family' hotels; 'mission' hotels *(missionshoteller)*, which are really a special type of family hotel; country inns (the very distinctive word for inn is *kro*); and guesthouses.

The more expensive hotels are naturally plentiful in main towns and resorts. De luxe prices are fairly high—in Copenhagen you must reckon to pay up to 250 kr or more a night per double room including 2 breakfasts. For full board you will pay 220—350 kr per person. In more modest Copenhagen hotels reckon on paying 90—100 kr for a double room without bath but including breakfasts. Prices, however, even in the capital, go as low as 60 kr for bed and breakfast.

All prices quoted are fully inclusive—*MOMS,* service, and everything else. Outside Copenhagen prices work out at a little more than half those of the capital.

Denmark's 'mission' hotels are in reality a special type of family concern. Though all carry the same title they are not parts of a vast chain, but are individually run—often by families who have owned the hotel for perhaps two or three generations. All have a religious and temperance background. In most you will notice nothing out of the ordinary except a bible—in Danish—discreetly placed in every room and a notice telling you when morning prayers are held should you wish to attend. 'Temperance' to Danes means the serving of wines and beers, but nothing stronger.

Not the least of the mission hotels' advantages is that they are usually appreciably cheaper than comparable ordinary hotels. As a result they are apt to be heavily booked—in Copenhagen throughout the year, and in other places at Christmas, Easter, and during the Danish school summer holidays which last from mid-June to the end of August.

Inns Many inns are extremely attractive old buildings, with facilities completely up to date. As bases for touring and for activities such as fishing they can be ideal. Except in one or two that have become specially popular, prices are relatively low.

Overnight stays need to be booked in advance but midday and evening meals are always available. If you are driving through Denmark and want to eat well you can rarely do better than to pull up at a place marked *Kro*.

Motels Modern motels also cater for motorists. Some that are located just outside big towns, including Copenhagen, provide good accommodation at rates that may be lower than inside the city limits. Places described as 'motels' provide genuine facilities specially designed for motorists, usually with a petrol station and garage which does repairs next door to them.

Guesthouses in Denmark vary from establishments which are in reality small family-run hotels to private families who let bedrooms and provide breakfast and sometimes other meals during the summer. Some larger establishments of the first type are included in hotel lists supplied free by the Danish National Tourist Office, but addresses of the smaller places can be obtained only from local Tourist Offices. The accommodation provided is usually of a very high standard, but prices do not always strike British visitors as being particularly low.

Youth hostels Denmark has 84 Youth Hostels in Copenhagen and strategic positions throughout the country. Standards are in general very high. Dormitory accommodation for men and women is available, but much of the space in modern hostels is used for rooms containing 4 beds which can also be used by families. Youth Hostel membership is not restricted by age, nor do you have to leave the car at home when you stay at the hostels. Youth Hostel tours by car, cycle, or bus are very popular with the Danes themselves. The family rooms are available to any parents with children under 15. Overnight stays cost roughly 7—10 kr depending on the hostel: cooked meals can be bought cheaply in most hostels. (9 kr per main meal, 6.50 kr for large breakfast, 1.50 kr each for sandwiches). Membership of your own national Youth Hostels association is necessary unless you buy an international guest card at one of the country's larger hostels or at the headquarters office, Herbergs-Ringen, Vesterbrogade 35, DK-1620 Copenhagen V.

Special dormitory accommodation, costing 15—25 kr, is available in Copenhagen during the summer. Information can be obtained from the Tourist Information Office. More primitive 'sleep-ins' are also provided, costing about 10 kr a night. Information about these is provided by the Youth Information Centre at Raadhusstræde 13.

Sleeping overnight in parks is forbidden. If you attempt it the police will remove you.

Farmhouse holidays A particular form of private house accommodation that has proved enormously popular with visitors from Britain and other countries is the holiday organised in farmhouses by a number of regional associations, mainly in Jutland and on Funen island. In Britain these are marketed quite cheaply by DFDS and other travel firms (for addresses see p 18), though it is also possible, if you have any special reason for it and are prepared to spend the extra time or money, to make the arrangements yourself.

Guests rarely total more than 6—8. While holidaymakers are completely free to do as they please, there is nothing to stop them from joining in the farm's activities—and these often turn out the holiday's main attraction, especially with children. In most cases weekend visits to Copenhagen are organised at extremely attractive rates, and even families with small children find they can leave them happily with their farmer hosts.

Furnished chalets These are little bungalows, often built of wood and frequently very small indeed, usually sited within easy reach of a good beach. Many of the chalets are small, but efficiently fitted: many nowadays are thoroughly comfortable. A number of British travel firms offer inclusive-price holidays in selected chalets suitably close to shops and entertainments.

You can also arrange lettings direct with Danish families or firms, but because some concerns have proved unreliable the Danish National Tourist Office suggests that you make preliminary enquiries either through local Tourist Offices or to a recommended firm in Copenhagen which lets chalets in all parts of the country—Dansk Centralkontor for Sommerhus-Udlejning A/S, Falkoneralle 7, DK-2000 Copenhagen F.

Campsites Denmark has some of the best and best-organised campsites in Europe. Over 500 of them have been inspected and approved by the Danish camping federation. They are divided into 1, 2, and 3-star categories. The 1-star camps must all possess the essential minimum of sanitary installations, drinking water, and so on. 2-star sites possess in addition windbreaks, showers, laundry facilities, and a provision store within 2 km. Places awarded 3 stars have everything, and many are so luxuriously equipped that they even stay open the whole year. Overnights at Danish campsites cost up to about 7.00 kr.

An international camping carnet, obtainable by members from motoring organisations, the Camping Club of Great Britain, the Caravan Club, and other associations, is necessary, though you can also buy an emergency Danish camping pass at the first approved site you visit. It costs 4 kr and covers the holder and his family for 4 weeks on all approved sites. At some sites visitors can hire tents and equipment.

Though it is simpler to use an organised site you can camp also on private land, provided you obtain permission first. Farms on the island of Mors in North Jutland specialise in accepting campers. Details can be obtained from the Tourist Information Office in Nykøbing Mors. A certain number of sites are run by the Danish motoring organisation known by its initials FDM. These are open to all members of the AA and RAC.

A free summarised list of selected campsites is available from the Danish National Tourist Office. The full detailed list of sites can be bought from motoring organisations, at the frontier, or from Dansk Central Boghandel, Nørregade 49, DK-1165, Copenhagen K.

Electricity 220 volts AC and 50 cycles are normal almost everywhere in Denmark. In a few places however you may find supplies at 110 or 220 volts DC. Do not connect an AC electric shaver or other AC appliance to a DC circuit.

Laundry and dry-cleaning Hotels will normally look after guests' laundry and dry-cleaning, and guesthouses and campsite wardens will tell you where you can get things washed or cleaned. Prices are mostly somewhat higher than in Britain. The better campsites have ironing-rooms and irons for guests' use.

Taking the children Denmark is an ideal country for family holidays, however young the children may be. Hygiene standards are, to be blunt, much higher than Britain's. Pasteurised milk is readily available in the shops, along with all the baby foods we are accustomed to. Hotels provide cots, and both hotel restaurants and others supply high chairs, baby plates and cutlery, special foods, and even feeding-bottles as a matter of course. Many hotels also have well equipped children's playrooms. Responsible English-speaking babysitters can usually be produced at 2 or 3 hours' notice: the normal charge is about 20 kr per hour. Children's facilities abound. (For train travel facilities see p 8; for junk playgrounds see p 68).

Restaurants and Snackbars

You will find large numbers of restaurants in all the larger towns, in the main tourist areas, and also on all ferries serving the longer sea-routes. Snackbars (*cafeterias*) are also frequent in towns and tourist regions.

It should be remembered however that if Danes go to a restaurant for lunch or dinner it is usually a slap-up meal that they want..

Helpings are enormous, and prices fairly high though not excessive. Allow 70—80 kr a head, including wine or other drinks.

Finding meals which are less expensive depends largely on knowing the Danes' eating habits: these are discussed more fully on p 76. Here we can only say that places serving a Danish 'cold table' *(kolde bord)* often offer excellent bargains. A 'cold table' does not consist entirely of cold food: it normally includes a huge choice of *smørrebrød* (Danish open sandwiches), a choice of hot dishes, and cheese, fruit, and possibly other desserts. You serve yourself and eat as much as you want.

The cold table at Copenhagen's Central Station is deservedly famous. It provides a choice of 60 open sandwiches, 4 or 5 hot dishes, cheese, fruit, and desserts for 23 kr (about £1.55 at current exchange rates). Other big stations also have good restaurants: in a strange place they are good spots to make for.

If you want a full restaurant meal, but do not wish to pay too much, ask for the 'daily card' *(daglig kort)*, not the 'menu'. The daily card gives details of the table d'hôte meal—a limited number of choices for each course but at a lower price than if ordered à la carte. 'Menu' to a Dane means the à la carte list.

Cheaper dishes and snacks can be obtained in snackbars, though you need a certain amount of personal experience in deciding what you find satisfying among the reasonably-priced dishes.

Another possibility, not to be despised even though it may strike you at first as undignified, is to buy frankfurters *(pølser)* from a stall.

Bars and Nightspots

Cafés and bars where you can order drinks and sit and talk or just sit and watch the world go by, are plentiful enough in towns and holiday areas. Coffee, chocolate, and tea (which will be served English-fashion if you order it with milk and ask for it to be served strong) are available as well as alcoholic drinks. Prices are mostly well above British standards, especially for things like beer and whisky. Nice girls usually do not go unaccompanied to bars in Copenhagen's Vesterbrogade and Nyhavn areas, but elsewhere they can do as they please.

All major towns and holiday areas, including especially Copenhagen, are well provided with night entertainment which ranges from dinner-dance establishments where formal clothes are essential, to discothèques, jazz clubs and other places where music is the chief attraction—and to noisy, lively spots which may be thoroughly well conducted or cheerfully disreputable.

The Copenhagen leaflet available free from the National Tourist Office lists the capital's better-known nightspots and tells you clearly what to expect from each. Elsewhere you can get up-to-date information from the local Tourist Office or your hotel porter or receptionist. In several large provincial capitals, as well as Copenhagen, you can drink or drink and dance right through the night until the first bars open next morning. Because of high drink prices evenings of this sort are however apt to seem a little expensive to British visitors.

Shopping

Excursions into Danish shops are pure joy—provided your purse is long enough. Furniture, silverware, ceramics, toys, textiles, furs, and all sorts of other items are beautifully and entertainingly designed and made. Jensen silver, Royal Copenhagen porcelain, Bing & Grøndal ceramics—these are among the country's world-famous products. Denmark's skill in toymaking is less clearly appreciated— until you realise that Lego and trolls are just two of many items the Danes have given the world's children. Danish furniture has qualities of design all its own, and here, too, many individual items have become known all over the world—Arne Jacobsen's single-skin leather armchair, for instance, and Kare Klint's folded lampshades. When it comes to small souvenir items—little figures, tiny candlesticks, and the like—the Danes are supreme. Nor is Copenhagen by any means the only town with a worthwhile shopping centre.

Tourists who have goods dispatched direct to their homes by the shops are not obliged to pay *MOMS* (VAT), which reduces the price by about 13%. Many large shops undertake to dispatch goods. If you arrange for this to be done ask to see evidence of insurance for breakable or valuable items, and keep the firm's name and address and receipt in a safe place until after delivery.

If you are shopping for food you will find quality excellent and service usually thoroughly efficient and helpful. Prices (for details see p 17) are either the same as Britain's or a trifle higher—except for fish, which is mostly decidedly cheap. Tea bags, but not British-style packet teas, can be bought, but are rather more expensive than in UK.

Shop opening times Normal hours are 09.00—17.30 on Monday to Friday, often with an extension to 19.00 on Friday. The majority of shops close at 13.00 on Saturday, though department stores usually stay open till 14.00. Confectioners and florists often open on Sundays and holidays, and some foodstores operate until 22.00 or later each night. Banks open 09.00—15.00 on Monday to Friday and also 16.00—18.00 on Friday. There is no Saturday opening.

15

Dresses

British	10	12	14	16	18	20
Continental	40	42	44	46	48	50

Shirts

British	13	13½	14	14½	15	15½	16	16½
Continental	33	34	36	37	38	39	41	42

Adult shoes

British	3	4	5	6	7	8	9	10
Continental	36	37	38	39	41	42	43	44

Glove, sock, and non-stretch tights sizes are the same as in the UK.

Weights and Measures
Weight The standard weight is the kilogram, which is approximately 2.2 lb.

Kilos	½	1	2	3	5	10	30	50	100	500
Pounds 9 oz	1.1	2.2	4.4	6.6	11	22	66	110	220	1100

Liquid The standard liquid measure is the litre, which equals approximately 1¾ pints. There are about 4½ litres to the gallon.

Litres	1	2	3	4	5	10	15	20	30	40	50
Gallons	.2	.4	.7	.9	1.1	2.2	3.3	4.4	6.6	8.8	11

Linear The standard measurement of length is the metre, which is 3 feet 3⅓ inches. There are 100 centimetres to the metre, and 1,000 metres to the kilometre, which is roughly equivalent to ⅝ of a mile.

Centimetres	1	2	3	4	5	10	25	50	100
Inches	.4	.8	1.2	1.6	2	3.9	9.8	19.7	39.4

Metres	1	2	3	4	5	10	25	50	100
Feet	3.3	6.6	9.8	13.1	16.4	32.8	82	164	328.1

Kms	1	5	10	20	50	100	200	300	400	500
Miles	.6	3.1	6.2	12.4	31.1	62.1	124.3	186.4	248.5	310.7

Shop prices As a rough guide, here are the prices that were being charged in spring 1974:

White bread (kg) 5-5.50 kr	Tea (100 g) 4.50 kr)
Butter (kg) 15 kr	Beer (bottle) 2 kr
Milk (litre) 2 kr	Soft drinks (bottle) 1-4 kr
Cheese (kg) 16 kr	Wine (bottle) 10-15 kr
Eggs (6) 4 kr	Aquavit (bottle) 40 kr
Fish (kg) 19-25 kr	Imported whisky (bottle) 60 kr
Ham (kg, tinned) 29 kr	British cigarettes (20) 9 kr
Coffee (kg) 31 kr	Danish cigarettes (20) 8.60 kr

Drinks in bars and restaurants
Coffee (cup) 2.50-3.50 kr (pot) 5-8 kr; Tea (pot) 5-8 kr; Beer (bottle) 4-6 kr; Milk (glass) 2 kr; Soft drinks (bottle) 3-4.50 kr; Aquavit (glass) 4.50-6 kr; Imported whisky (large nip) 7-12 kr; Danish liqueurs (glass) 6-8 kr; Wine (bottle) 28-36 kr.

Emergency and General Information

If you have booked an inclusive holiday, your travel firm's rep will normally give any help you need. In other cases consult your hotel or the local tourist office. Do not overlook the uses of credit cards (Diners, Access, Barclaycard and so on), or of bank cards.

British Consuls and Vice-Consuls are not allowed to give you any assistance beyond returning you to Britain by the cheapest method if you cannot pay for your own tickets, and getting you a temporary travel document if you have lost your passport. They will, however, give advice and general information in the event of serious difficulty, such as arrest by the police.

Postal Services

		Denmark	UK & Europe	N. America
Postcards	(surface)	0.60	—	—
	(by air)	—	0.60	0.60
Letters	(surface)	0.70	—	—
	(air: up to 5g)	—	1 kr	1 kr
Telegrams	(minimum +	—	8 kr (min) +	8 kr (min) +
	per word)		1.30 kr per wd	3.40 kr per wd

Stamps can be bought at post offices, kiosks which sell postcards, and hotel reception desks. Post offices normally open from 09.00 to 17.30 Mon.-Sat., except for the one at Copenhagen's Central Station, which opens from 08.00 to 23.00 Mon.-Sat. and 08.00 to 21.00 Sun.

Telephone calls from automatic boxes cost 0.25 kr per 3 minutes for internal calls. Calls to UK cost 3 kr per 1 min and to USA 18 kr (14 kr from 22.00 to 10.00).

Churches

Church of England—St Alban's Church, Churchillparken, Copenhagen: also occasional services in Aarhus

Methodists—churches throughout the country: information from Centralmissionen, Stokhusgade 2, DK-1317 Copenhagen S

Roman Catholics—many churches throughout the country, with services in Danish: for foreign language services write to Katolsk Bispenkontor, Bredgade 69A, DK-1260 Copenhagen F, or enquire from tourist offices or hotels.

National holidays New Year's Day (January 1st), Maundy Thursday, Good Friday, Easter Sunday, Easter Monday, 'Store Bededag' (Great Prayer Day—normally the 4th Friday after Easter), Ascension Day, Whit Sunday, Whit Monday, Constitution Day (June 5th), Christmas period (from noon on December 24th up to and including December 26th).

Tipping Railway and ferry porters expect about 2 kr for each piece of luggage carried, or perhaps a little more. The only other people you tip are provincial taxi-drivers with non-inclusive meters (15%). Do not attempt to tip where tipping is not expected: it may be considered an insult, and you may in any case suffer the embarrassment of having the tip handed back.

WCs There are public lavatories—marked WC (pronounced Vee-See) or *Toiletter*—in some public places. Elsewhere go into any bar or restaurant or hotel. A charge may be made of 0.25 to 1 kr: if none is specified you do not pay.

Addresses

In Britain

Information:

Danish National Tourist Office, Sceptre House, 169-173 Regent Street, London W1R 8PY (handles enquiries of all sorts, not only those directly connected with tourism)

Royal Danish Consulate-General, 67 Pont Street, London S.W.1

Danish Institute, 3 Doune Terrace, Edinburgh 3 (for information about cultural matters, history, etc)

Motoring and personal insurance:

AA, PO Box 50, Basingstoke, Hants RG21 2ED

Caravan Club, 65 South Molton Street, London W1Y 2AB

Camping Club of Great Britain, 11 Lower Grosvenor Place, London SW1W 0EY

Europ Assistance, 269-273 High Street, Croydon, Surrey CR0 1QH

Holiday organisers:

Bennett Travel, 48 Wigmore Street, London W1

DFDS Travel, 8 Berkeley Square, London W1

Scantours, 8 Spring Gardens, London SW1

These companies are all specialists in travel in Denmark, including farmhouse holidays, cycling tours, and chalet holidays. Bookings can be made without extra charge through any ABTA-member travel agent (look for the sign on the window). British Airways also run Freewheeler holidays in Denmark (2 people travelling by air pay little or nothing for a hired car).

Independent travel and ferry bookings:
DFDS Seaways, 8 Berkeley Square, London W1
British Airways, West London Air Terminal, London SW7 4ED
S.A.S. Scandinavian Airlines, 52-3 Conduit Street,
   London W1R 0AY
Sealink Car Ferry Centre, PO Box 305, 52 Grosvenor Gardens,
   London SW1W 0AG
British Rail Continental, PO Box 2, Victoria Station,
   London SW1V 6YL
British Air Ferries, Municipal Airport, Southend-on-Sea,
   Essex SS2 6YL

In Denmark
British Embassy and Consulate-General, 38-40 Kastelsvej,
   DK-2100, Copenhagen Ø: there are also Vice-Consuls in
   Aabenraa, Aalborg, Aarhus, Esbjerg, and Odense
British Airways, Vesterbrogade 2b, Copenhagen
S.A.S., Royal Hotel Air Terminal, Hammerichsgade, Copenhagen
DFDS (HQ), Sankt Annæ Plads 30, DK-1250, Copenhagen K

Charges

Sport
Golf up to 34 kr green fee
Tennis up to 10 kr per hour
Riding 15—20 kr per hour
Sailing and boating up to 1800 kr per week
Sea-fishing 3 kr
Lake and river fishing 2—10 kr per day
Bathing—Denmark has no private beaches and no charges are made for sea bathing: swimming pools cost 2—5 kr.

Motoring
Petrol per litre—from 2.20 kr (ordinary) to 2.26 kr (super)
Oil per litre 4.50 kr
Parking up to 1 kr per hour

Museum and art gallery opening times and charges
Most galleries and museums are open from 10.00 to 16.00 or 17.00, but there can be considerable variations. Copenhagen's National Museum, for example, opens different sections on different days.

If a gallery or museum closes at all during the week it is usually on Monday. Admission charges, if made at all, range normally from 1 to 5 kr (occasionally more, but not often) for adults, with children often admitted free.

Rudkøbing (see p 51)

Motoring and Cycling in Denmark

Motoring in Denmark is pleasant for a number of reasons. Apart from 4 or 5 big towns and one or two main through-routes traffic is rarely heavy. Inns *(kroen)* make attractive stopping-places for meals or coffee. The rolling countryside, with its trim farms, woods, and heathland is much more colourful than Britons usually imagine. Except in Copenhagen, accommodation is easy to find: if nothing is available where you decide to stop people send you on a few miles— and phone ahead to make certain beds are available. Motorists visiting Copenhagen in high season should however book weeks or even months ahead. The alternative is to stay outside the capital —at Roskilde, say, or somewhere like Hellebæk on the coast north of Copenhagen.

DFDS ferry services to Esbjerg have normal drive-on facilities. Car and passenger rates are given on p 6. For shorter sea-crossings use the ferry services to Ostend from Harwich, Dover, or Folkestone. British Air Ferries can also take you and your car from Ashford (Kent) to Ostend.

If you are considering a circular tour that includes other countries as well as Denmark ask DFDS (address on p 18) for details of their 'Captain's Card' tickets. For a single inclusive payment these permit you and your car to use an extraordinarily wide choice of Scandinavian and Scandinavian-UK ferry routes.

Vehicle documents To drive a car or ride a motorcycle or moped in Denmark you need a full (not provisional) British driving licence, the vehicle's registration certificate ('log book'), and a 'green card' certificate of international insurance. You obtain this last from your own insurance company who will charge you a small fee. It extends to specified countries outside the UK the cover provided by your existing policy. Apply at least 2 or 3 weeks before departure. If the vehicle you are taking to Denmark is not your own you must have a letter of authority from the owner and a photocopy of the log book if you are not carrying the original. The minimum age for driving a motor vehicle in Denmark is 18.

While the green card provides the legally required third-party insurance and, if comprehensive, gives also cover for your own vehicle it is highly advisable to take out extra insurance against the costs of extra hotel accommodation, etc (see p 3).

Laws In Denmark you drive on the right. This presents no problem provided you take the first hour or two gently. The most dangerous moments occur when pulling out from a garage or roadside stop. Try always to pull up on the road's right hand side, so that you are less likely to drive off instinctively on the left hand side.

Headlights One Danish law requires action before departure. Left-dipping headlights are illegal. You are permitted to tape over the part of the headlight through which the leftward beam passes, but it is much more effective to fit yellow, right hand dipping lenses obtainable from garages, motor accessory shops, and elsewhere.

Penalties for driving under the influence of drink are extremely heavy. A specially light beer *(lys øl)*, which tastes very pleasant, is manufactured for drivers. At dinners and other gatherings you can prevent people serving you alcohol by simply placing your glass upside down in front of you.

Speed limits Denmark has no general speed limits—only local restrictions indicated (in kilometres of course) by the normal international signs. Cars towing caravans are however limited to 70 km per hour (44 mph).

Overtaking is forbidden if it involves crossing even a single white line, and also at approaches to pedestrian crossings. Indicators are not normally used to show that you intend to overtake—you perform the whole operation without signals.

Priority rules are different from Britain's. Basically you give way to all traffic coming from your right. This rule is strictly applied at roundabouts, where vehicles joining have priority. On main roads, however, vehicles using minor approach roads give way to other traffic. Cars must always give way to buses pulling out from stops.

Parking is prohibited on motorways, main roads, and immediately before pedestrian crossings. Elsewhere it is normally permitted, but not if the car is facing the 'wrong' way. Special regulations apply in towns. Some parts of Copenhagen are equipped with parking meters, but in most places the disc system is used. You get a disc from a police station, post office, garage, bank, or elsewhere and set it to the time at which you leave the car. This shows whether you have exceeded the permitted parking time.

The Danish word for hour is *time* (plural *timer*) and the international 'P' parking sign with, say, *2 timer* means you can stay 2 hours. *Parkeringforbudt* indicates that parking is forbidden. *Stopforbudt* means you must not stop for any purpose whatsoever. In some towns you may also come across a notice saying *Datoparkering*. Here you park on one or other side of the road according to the date: if you do not understand the sign clearly, park on the same side as all the other cars there. Parked cars must be locked and the handbrake applied.

Traffic lights operate as in Britain. Flashing red lights are used at level crossings and occasionally for other obstructions. A flashing amber light means 'proceed—but with caution'.

In towns, and especially in Copenhagen, pedestrians are obliged to cross only at official crossings or as directed by policemen. This rule is usually strictly obeyed when traffic is heavy. A number of towns have cycle tracks, raised slightly above main road level, at the roadway's outer edges. They are sometimes separated from the roadway by a white line, but are often very difficult indeed to distinguish at night. In towns cyclists are often numerous, and not always very respectful of other traffic.

Accident procedure is fundamentally the same as in Britain, except that it is normal to allow the other driver to copy your name and address and your insurance company's name and address from formal documents rather than to write them down for him. Your UK driving licence and insurance certificate show this information very clearly. Call the police and obtain witnesses (if possible).

Breakdowns AA and RAC members can obtain free breakdown assistance on motorways and numbered main roads from FDM or KDAK patrols (FDM and KDAK are the Danish motoring organisations corresponding to the AA and RAC). The usual plan however is to phone, or get someone else to phone, the remarkable Falck organisation, which not only provides car breakdown services throughout Denmark but also operates the country's fire brigades and ambulance services, as well as much of its insurance. Falck's services are not free, but have the advantage that one of their patrol vehicles is never more than a few miles away.

Roads and signposts Denmark's roads, even very minor ones, are usually well surfaced and of very good construction. Motorways, for which no toll is charged, link the busiest towns, and a huge number of car-carrying ferries make it possible to reach even the smallest and remotest islands quickly. Bridges link most larger islands, and one to Sweden has been planned.

Destination signs mostly follow international patterns. On the open road signposting is clear and efficient. In towns however destination boards are sometimes placed so low that cars and people hide them completely, and sometimes they are positioned so that you drive through a crossroads before discovering you ought to have turned right.

Roads are numbered and the numbers shown clearly both on signposts and on maps. Main roads carry the prefix 'A' and motorways 'M'. On minor roads the simple finger-posts are usually efficient enough to prevent you losing your way.

A number of road signs tend to use words. Those worth knowing include:

Spærret—   Road Closed

Halve Vejbane Spærret—	Road closed over half its width— traffic in one direction only
Ensrettet—	One-Way Street (traffic in direction of arrow)
Cyklesti—	Cycle Track (for cycles and mopeds only)
Cyklesti Ender—	Cycle Track ends (most important: here cyclists pour out on to the road)
Rabatten Blød or Rabatten er Blød—	Soft Verge
Vejarbejde—	Road Works in Progress
Omkørsel—	Diversion
Kun Personvogne	Private Cars Only

One special emblem sign that you may see occasionally in woodlands is a simple solid red disc. It means 'no road for cars', though cyclists can still use the track.

Ferry bookings In summer bookings are essential on Great Belt ferry services and advisable on most other routes. The Danish National Tourist Office provides (free) a booklet listing all car ferries in Danish waters and telling you where to make advance reservations for each. Many are run by Danish Railways: bookings for these can be made at any railway station.

Cycling Cycling is popular in Denmark: whole families often go touring on holiday together. Many minor roads and woodland tracks are ideal for cycling, and towns also often provide special tracks, separated from other traffic. A dozen or so main railway stations, including some in Copenhagen suburbs, hire bikes for around 10 kr a day, with a deposit of 25 kr. Before hiring you must prove your identity—eg by showing your passport (but not leaving it).

Individually packaged cycle-touring holidays can also be bought from certain travel agencies and from the Tourist Information Offices in Svendborg, Vejle, Viborg, and Aarhus. Accommodation and everything else is pre-arranged, but you can start the trip on any day you wish.

Maps If you intend going only to Copenhagen and a few other large cities almost any road map of Denmark will serve you well enough. If, however, you want to tour and get to know the countryside, the 10 maps published by the Geodætisk Institut on a scale of 1:150,000 (about 2¼ miles to 1 inch) are ideal: you'll find them among Europe's best touring maps. They can be bought easily in Danish bookshops and also from British motoring organisations or from the map and guidebook specialists, Edward Stanford Ltd, 12 Long Acre, London WC2E 9LP.

Attractive touring regions Provided you do not spend all your time on motorways most of Denmark offers pleasant touring. The areas with the most enjoyable changes of scenery are: the Rebild Hills, the Silkeborg Hills and lakes, the fjords and hills spread almost all along east Jutland's coast, the south Funen Hills, northern Zealand, and the island of Bornholm.

Some basic distances (in km) From Kolding, at the intersection of the main east-west A1 (Esbjerg-Kolding-Odense-Copenhagen) and the main south-north Jutland highway, A10:

Esbjerg—73   Krusaa (German frontier)—72
Aarhus—73   Odense—53
Aalborg (via Aarhus)—185   Copenhagen (via Odense, excluding
                                   Great Belt ferry)—188

Other important distances from Copenhagen are:
Helsingør—45   Rødbyhavn (via K øge)—151
Køge—38   Sjællands Odde (fo · short ferry to
                                   Ebeltoft and Jutl ind)—116

What to See

It is only in recent years that ordinary British holidaymakers have begun to appreciate fully what Denmark offers. While none of the hills are of any great height the landscapes almost everywhere lack the flatness that Britons used to attribute to Denmark. Many areas, such as southern Funen, the east Jutland coast, the Rebild Hills, and parts of Bornholm island have slopes that the most energetic cyclist or walker will find provide an adequate day's exercise. And the cliffs on Møn and Bornholm islands and on the Stevn peninsula are striking enough as scenery for anyone's taste.

But whatever you start by looking for in Denmark, you usually end by enjoying the countryside's extraordinary peacefulness, the liveliness and attractiveness of the towns, and the sheer friendliness and helpfulness of almost everyone you meet. You can drive peacefully on most second-tier main roads, and if you set out to get away from it all you can cycle all day and see only half a dozen motor vehicles. Industry came relatively late to Denmark, and when it arrived the Danes had already learnt to make even industrial towns attractive. There are not many countries where 'Gasworks Avenue' turns out to be one of the best addresses in town—but it happens in Denmark. In this country too you can rely on virtually everyone being ready to give you a hand when you need it, whether he is paid to do so or not.

Every first-time visitor to Denmark will want to see Copenhagen. It is indeed one of Europe's most delightful cities. But, as happens with most capitals, you do not really get to know either the country or its people unless you get out into the villages and smaller towns and the remoter spots. Thanks to Denmark's excellent roads, transport services, and innumerable ferries this is very easy.

Copenhagen

Even before World War II Denmark's capital city enjoyed a well deserved reputation for liveliness, gaiety, colour, and good taste—and recent years have enhanced it. During long summer days, when the sun seems hardly to set at all, its palaces and gardens, colourful old buildings, elegant shops, and bustling seafront make it a wonderful centre for holidaymakers. And even on grey, possibly cold, winter days, when daylight lasts only a few hours, life continues as gay as ever in the city's lively restaurants and nightspots, its bars and theatres and shops. But you must not get the idea that Copenhageners think of nothing but pleasure. One of the city's most extraordinary aspects is that its inhabitants work at least as hard as they play.

Copenhagen today is a bustling modern city. Including adjacent suburbs that are legally separate communities, it is the home of over 1½ million people, more than a quarter of Denmark's entire population. The suburbs' beautifully-designed houses and flats, gay in summer with flowers on windowsills as well as in gardens, are particularly striking, and so are many of the modern office blocks and hotels. But the relatively tiny centre still boasts many enchanting old buildings—sometimes whole streets of them—and winding narrow thoroughfares. Straddling a strait between the larger island of Zealand (Sjælland) and smaller Amager it has the sea right in its heart. And that gives the town a very special atmosphere.

If you want to enjoy the town fully you must do it on foot or by bicycle. Taxi or organised coach tours give a quick glimpse of its main items, but using your own car is not advisable because of one-way streets, and parking problems.

One of the old streets, Copenhagen

The Central Station *(Hovedbanegaard)* makes a good starting point. Its buildings include the Danish Tourist Board's information office (on the left of the station's Vesterbrogade entrance), the city's Accommodation Bureau (Kiosk P, main booking hall), and a famous restauı nt which provides Denmark's (and probably the world's) best D nish 'cold table'.

Opposite the stɑ ion's Vesterbrogade ('West Bridge Street') exit a column in the middle of the road commemorates the liberation of Denmark's serfs in 1788. Turn left down the road and you will come to more modern emancipation in one of the turnings in the form of a riotous collection of sex shops, porn shops, and tarts for every type and taste. In the opposite direction, on the further side from the railway, you come soon to one of Europe's most delightful shops. Called *'Den Permanente'* (short for 'The Permanent Exhibition of Arts and Crafts'), it is a sort of designers' retail outlet. All products are eligible provided they satisfy an expert selection committee: many of Denmark's most famous firms, such as silversmith Georg Jensen and Royal Copenhagen Porcelain, exhibit there though they have their own shops for sales.

Further on, on Vesterbrogade's other side, you reach the world-famous Tivoli Gardens' main entrance. Laid out beside a selection of the old city moat in 1843 Tivoli has grown into a sort of summary of the entire Danish character. The gardens themselves are beautiful. They contain elegant and exotic and fanciful buildings, all of them very colourful. Entertainments range from a big dipper to a famous marionette theatre, from riotous music hall shows to top-class ballet programmes, symphony concerts and chamber music. You can eat at hot dog *(pølser)* stalls or some of Copenhagen's best and most elegant restaurants.

There is a children's playground, dancing, and community singing—or you can just sit and admire the flowers and the lights. The Tivoli Boy Guards, modelled on the Royal Guard, and their highly skilled band perform on Saturday and Sunday evenings. Firework nights (Wed 23.15, Sat and Sun 23.45) are magnificent. Only Denmark could revel in such a mixture of simplicity and sophistication. Admission costs 1.50 to 4.00 kr according to time and day of week, but thousands of Copenhageners buy season tickets: the gardens are open May 1st to September 16th only.

A few seconds' more walk along Vesterbrogade brings you into Town Hall Square *(Raadhuspladsen)*, the city's busiest traffic centre. You can go round the extremely handsome Town Hall, completed in 1905. Apart from elegant staircases, frescos, painting, and statuary, it contains a remarkable astronomical clock which started working in 1955. It tells the time by various methods, and gives moon phases, star movements, the dates of Easter and other 'movable' Christian feasts—and even incorporates a calendar valid for the next 500,000 years.

A hotel, offices, shops, restaurants, bars, and even an English-style pub are scattered round the square. And opposite Vesterbrogade a string of northward-leading narrow streets, now closed to traffic and known collectively as *Strøget* ('The Strip'), constitutes a major and much loved centre of Copenhagen life. This is the heart of the old town. Some of its houses date back several centuries. Strøget's sides are lined with jostling cinemas, bars, souvenir markets, and elegant shops—Georg Jensen, Bing & Grøndahl, and Royal Copenhagen Porcelain for instance. It passes through the adjacent Gammeltorv and Nytorv Squares (Old Market and New Market), flanks the Church of the Holy Ghost (14th century, rebuilt 1720), with its simple monument to an unknown Danish concentration camp victim, and after almost a mile deposits you in Kongens Nytorv (King's New Square—it is actually circular).

Across the square the Royal Theatre, three theatres in one, is the home of Denmark's Royal Ballet as well as its national theatre company. The Danish Royal Ballet is Western Europe's oldest and one of its best: the earliest item in its repertory dates from 1786. Beside the Royal Theatre the impressive 17th-century mansion called Charlottenborg houses the Royal Academy of Arts. And just beyond it you find the street and waterway called Nyhavn (New Harbour). Once a rowdy seamen's quarter it has become respectable, but still lively, in recent years. It includes some good restaurants, bars, and shops.

Nyhavn is a genuine part of the city's old harbour area. North of it, Amaliengade leads you to the charming rococo royal palace of Amalienborg (built 1754-60). It consists of four identical houses, originally intended for aristocratic families, arranged round a square, and is normally the royal family's summer home. In the little park north of Amalienborg you will see the English-looking church spire projecting above the trees belongs to St Alban's English church. The double-moated fort beyond it that once guarded the harbour has now been handed over to squatters of all ages in a unique social experiment.

Beyond the fort's main entrance and the ornate Gefion fountain (1907) you reach the sea at the lovely Langelinie Promenade. Here you find colourful restaurants, the Royal Danish Yacht Club, and, perched on a boulder, the famous Little Mermaid (Den lille Havefrue) of Hans Andersen's story, forever looking across the sea to the shipyards on the further island of Amager.

A left turn off Strøget at Gammeltorv takes us to the university quarter, with its bookshops, antique dealers, and boutiques

(Studiestræde and Fiolstræde), and the Regensen student hostel originally built by Christian IV with his observatory Round Tower *(Rundtaarn)* opposite it in Krystalgade. Peter the Great of Russia rode his horse up the tower's internal ramp, intended for heavy astronomical equipment.

Christian IV also designed and built Holy Trinity Church (Trinitatis Kirke) behind the tower and the charming renaissance mansion called Rosenborg a few hundred yards north, where he died in 1648. In his day it was a country house outside the city's ramparts. Now, surrounded by Kongens Have ('King's Garden') it houses the Crown Jewels and a museum of royal relics. Off Skindergade, near Regensen, you will find Graabrødretorv (Greyfriars Square), lined with delightful, bright-hued 16th-17th century houses.

A right turn off Strøget at the end of Amagertorv brings you through Højbroplads to Gammelstrand (Old Beach: some good restaurants here), with Slotsholmen (The Castle Island) reached by a bridge across the sea canal. Slotsholm contains Christiansborg Castle, the Thorvaldsen Museum, the Royal Library, the Armoury Museum (Tøjhusmuseet), the highly decorative Stock Exchange designed and built by Christian IV (how did he come to think up the spire of twisted dragons' tails?), and the elegant little naval

Copenhagen: the spire of the Stock Exchange in the foreground, with the Christiansborg Palace immediately behind

Holmens Kirke (The Island's Church), converted from an anchor forge by the architect-king. Modern (1916) despite its appearance, Christiansborg houses the Danish Parliament (Folketing), numerous ministries, and the powerful Ombudsmand's unpretentious office, open to any complainant without even an appointment, beside the Folketing. Traces of Copenhagen's earliest building, the castle raised by Bishop Absalon 800 years ago, can also be seen in Christiansborg (apply main entrance).

With its varied buildings and charming gardens Slotsholmen can easily occupy a day's sightseeing. You could spend a further week in the National Museum beyond the canal just south of Christiansborg. Its collections cover the whole world.

Other specially notable museums and art galleries include the Ny Carlsberg Glyptotek (near the Central Station), northern Europe's finest collection of sculpture of all ages; the State Art Museum (Statens Kunstmuseum, near Rosenborg), a big general collection of paintings and drawings; the Museum of Applied Art (Kunstindustri Museum: near Amalienborg); and the Hirschsprung Gallery of paintings by Danish artists, bequeathed to the city in 1902 (near the State Art Museum).

South of the city centre you can visit the famous Carlsberg Brewery near the Zoo and the large Frederiksberg Have park that has some of Copenhagen's noisiest and liveliest restaurants and nightspots in nearby streets. Westward you reach the very modern Radio Building, Bellahøj hill with its vast trade fair and exhibition building, and the modernistic Grundtvig Church at Bispebjerg, built to honour the founder of the Folk High School movement.

Northward you come, inland, to a string of lakes where you can walk and cycle and make excursions by motorboat, to the charming little 18th-century Sorgenfri (Sans Souci) palace, and the great Frilandsmuseet (Open Air Museum) of re-erected old farms and village houses, started in 1901 and part of the National Museum. Along the coast you pass the Tuborg Brewery (which you can also visit), the vast wooded Charlottenlund park, Klampenborg's fine but very crowded Bellevue beach (Copenhageners call it 'The Fly Paper'), and its Dyrehave (Deer Park), a former royal hunting ground containing Eremitagen (The Hermitage)—originally a hunting lodge, and the well-patronised Bakken amusement park and funfair. You can reach all these places quickly by electric S-train *(S-tog)*, but a restful return route from Klampenborg in summer is by motorboat.

Motorboat ferries will also give you a relaxed trip from Nyhavn to the charming old harbour quarter of Christianshavn, which still preserves its canals and moated fortifications alongside the vast

The Deer Park

Burmeister & Wain works where half the world's merchant navy marine diesels are made and the baroque Vor Frelsers Kirke (Church of Our Saviour), with its elegant gilded spiral-staircase spire (which you can climb). Beyond Christianshavn lies the rest of Amager island, with Copenhagen's modern airport at Kastrup, the

Bakken: the largest amusement park in northern Europe

Amager Museum at Store Magleby where many Dutchmen settled in the 16th century, and a ferry port with fast links to Malmö in Sweden at Dragør.

Ferries cross from Havnegade to Malmö in Sweden (1½ hrs), from Dragør to Limhavn near Malmø (50 min), and from Tuborg Harbour to Landskrona, midway between Malmö and Hälsingborg (1¼ hrs). There are less frequent services to Travemünde in West Germany (8-8½ hours) and Oslo in Norway (15 hours).

Aabenraa

A pleasant small port town about 20 km north of the German frontier on the main road (A10) to North Jutland, Aabenraa lies at the head of an attractive fjord (the word in Danish means 'bay') on Jutland's hilly eastern side. It once handled important trade with Iceland and Baltic ports and is now a flourishing market town.

Aalborg

Denmark's fourth largest town, with a population approaching 100,000 excluding independent suburbs, Aalborg lies about 110 km south of Jutland's northern tip on the southern side of a branch of the Limfjord (see Mors) which cuts right through Northern Jutland, linking the North Sea to the Baltic. Noted mainly for its cement and tobacco manufactures and for its production of aquavit—Danes often use the term 'Aalborg' as an alternative to *snaps*—Aalborg is also an attractive holiday base with a delightful old centre.

This central area has been made into a traffic-free precinct. Its focal point is the delightful brick-built Gothic Cathedral, dating mainly from about 1500 in its present form and dedicated to the English seamen's patron saint St Boltolph. In Danish its name is Budolfi Kirke, and like all Danish churches its interior is colourful enough to surprise British and American visitors. Unusual wooden galleries line each side of the nave: the paintings on their panels include the arms of Christian VII of Denmark and the royal coat of arms of England: Christian's wife was an English princess. The pulpit is brightly coloured, as in most Danish churches. Some decorated pew ends date from 1739: others are more recent.

In Gammel Torv (Old Market) north of the Cathedral the town's delightful small Town Hall, little changed since it was built in 1762, stands in the north-east corner. Visitors are sometimes admitted: the baroque meeting-rooms upstairs are charming. In Budolfi Plads (St Botolph's Square) to the south the Aalborg Museum lies west of the Cathedral immediately beyond the fine Post Office building (with dovecots thoughtfully provided for the pigeons that were bound to settle there anyway). Along with an art collection the museum concentrates on local life and history, including important Viking relics.

The Monastery of the Holy Ghost (Helligaandsklostret) in C.W.Obels Plads behind the Post Office admits visitors to its delightful chapter house, refectory, and cellars. Built in 1432 to house monks and nuns and 60 ill or elderly people, it is Denmark's oldest publicly-supported charity.

In Østeraagade (just beyond the Town Hall: turn left) two fine old merchants' houses have been carefully preserved. The first, Jens Bangs Stenhus (Jens Bang's Brick House), is a magnificent 6-storey mansion dating from 1624, when bricks were still rare and luxurious. Jørgen Olufsens Gaard, a little further on, was timber-frame-built in 1616. Further down the road you reach the Aalborghus, a former royal castle overlooking the harbour and still used as an administrative centre: visitors are allowed into the charming 16th-century half-timbered courtyard.

Jens Bang's Brick House

In Vesterbro, parallel with Østeraagade west of the Budolfi Plads pedestrian precinct (you can reach it through Bispensgade, the town's main shopping centre), two fine groups of statuary typify the Danes' love of beauty and their readiness to spend public money on achieving it. Near the harbour the 'Cimbrian Bull', by Anders Bundgaard, recalls the Danish tribe from the nearby Himmerland region. Inland, near the Tourist Office, the Goose Girl, by Gerhard Henning, is even more famous.

Further inland still you come to the impressive Aalborghallen (The Aalborg Hall), dating from 1949. Aalborghallen contains over 800 rooms. The main assembly hall holds 3,400 people and can cope with anything from chamber music to a full-scale circus. Visitors can see over the complex when not in use.

Beyond the Aalborg Hall a series of parks includes the Møllepark and its zoo (some good restaurants in this area). Beyond them you come to Karolinelund, Aalborg's version of Copenhagen's Tivoli (see p 28). Algade and its continuations, running eastward from the Cathedral, contain a number of modest old one and two-storeyed timbered houses. In Nørresundby on the harbour's northern side, reached by a modern bridge, you find the vast Lindholm Høj Viking burial ground. It includes 140 'ship graves', tombs enclosed by standing stones making the outline shape of a boat.

Aarhus

Denmark's second city, her second busiest port (surpassed only by Esbjerg), large producer of beer, locomotives, vegetable oils, and refrigerators, university city and seat of a bishopric for over 1000 years, Aarhus is also an important holiday centre. It has fine parks, 15 km (9 miles) of excellent beaches north and south of the town, numerous hotels, restaurants, and nightspots, and an old city centre almost as charming as Aalborg's. In Denmark you have to accustom yourself to the idea that industrial cities can be also very beautiful.

The old town's centre is the Store Torv (Great Square), only a stone's throw from the harbour. The streets are winding and narrow here. A belt developed mainly in the 19th century surrounds this area. A by-pass road, part of the town's 20th-century planning, runs outside this region, about 1½ km (1 mile) from the Cathedral. Parks and cliffs at the by-pass's two ends and the hills and parks that flank it provide a very attractive layout.

On top of slopes dropping steeply to the shore north of the town the Risskov (or Riisskov: *skov* = wood) provides grazing for herds of deer under its beechwoods. Humans who go to stroll there can eat and drink well in the famous Sjette Frederiks Kro (Frederik VI Inn). Immediately below the slopes two enclosed bathing establishments, reserved for nude bathers, have been operating for generations. No one has ever bothered about the fact that you can see perfectly into them from above: the car park in fact is an ideal vantage point.

About 1½ km (1 mile) from the Frederik VI Inn the by-pass Ring Road (Ringgade) runs beside the University which was founded in 1928 and boasts many excellent modern buildings spread over the green hills. Another kilometre (¾ mile) brings you to the Botanical Gardens, laid out as a public park on the slope of another hill. At the bottom of the Gardens, on the town-centre (NE) side, you can walk without payment or formality into the charming open-air museum called Den gamle By (The Old Town: main entrance in Viborgvej). The Old Town consists of a delightful collection of genuine old houses re-erected to form an old town, with cobbled streets and a stream flowing through the middle. You can go into a number of buildings, filled with items typical of particular trades.

A whole complex of parks stretches along the hills and cliffs south of the town. First comes Frihede, with its zoo, nature trail, sports complex, and observatory. Then the Mindepark (Memorial Park), dedicated to Danes who died in World War I. From the Mindepark you can see Marselisborg Palace inland: it was given to King Christian X (1912-1947) by the people of Denmark and the public are not admitted. Marselisborg Skov and Storskov stretch for 8 km (5 miles) beyond the Mindepark. Here and on the beach, where the bathing is excellent, there are a number of pleasant restaurants.

In the town's old centre the main places of interest are the late-Gothic 15th-century brick-built Cathedral, the 12th-century Vor Frue Kirke (Church of Our Lady), Aarhus's oldest building and the town's original Cathedral, and the Aarhus Museum of art and antiquities. One of the museum's most striking exhibits is the so-called 'Grauballe Man', one of several accidentally mummified bodies discovered in Jutland bogs in modern times. They are believed to have been the voluntary victims of ritual sacrifices in the early centuries of the Christian era.

Just south of the old town centre Aarhus's impressive and very modern Town Hall (Raadhus) was one of the first buildings to make the name of the now world-famous architect-designer Arne Jacobsen. It was completed in 1942. Visitors are taken round in groups at fixed hours. The town's Tourist Office stands beside the Town Hall.

Ærøskøbing and Ærø island

Ærø island lies due south of Funen and its chief town and port, Ærøskøbing, is reached by ferry from Svendborg (see separate entry) in 1¼ hours.

Ærøskøbing

Ærøskøbing is widely appreciated as the most perfectly preserved of all Denmark's tiny old towns. Little more than a village in size its streets are still cobbled and lined with lovely, brightly-painted, tiny 17th-18th century timber-frame houses, gay with flowers in summer. We owe this little gem's continued existence mainly to Gunnar Hammerich, a sculptor who went to live in Ærøskøbing in 1916 and fought long and hard for its preservation. Astonishingly enough, he still lives there, and runs a delightful small museum in his own little house, called Hammerichs Hus.

Another little private museum, called in Danish Flaskeskibs-og Pibe Samling (usually translated as 'Bottle-Ship and Pipe Collection'), is perhaps more popular: it consists of hundreds of model ships in bottles and pipes from all over the world. But Ærøskøbing's real delight is simply strolling through its ancient, peaceful streets or sailing a yacht into its delightful small harbour.

A single main road runs Ærø island's whole length (about 25 km— 15 miles), through the villages that cluster on its central ridge. The pleasant rolling landscape is dotted with windmills. Marstal village, at Ærø's eastern end, still has a number of old houses. In the years before steam it was an important seafaring and shipbuilding centre. Its Maritime Museum recalls those days, and also displays a number of Stone Age grinding troughs and spherical grinding stones, all found locally, that are between 8,000 and 10,000 years old. A ferry connects Marstal to Rudkøbing on Langeland island in 1 hour (see Langeland).

Als island See Sønderborg.

Billund

If it seems strange that a Central Jutland village of 2000 inhabitants, 28 km west of Vejle, should have an airport capable of taking the world's largest jets, a 1st-class hotel, and an outstandingly good campsite, the reasons are not far to seek. The airport was built largely to handle worldwide charter air traffic for Europe's largest travel firm, built up in his spare time by Pastor Eilif Kroager, parish priest of Tjæreborg village near Esbjerg. The hotel and campsite cope with visitors to the vast entertainment centre called Legoland (pronounced Lee-golan in Danish).

The world-famous constructional toy Lego, today manufactured under licence in some 60 countries, was invented by the village carpenter's son in Billund. Now a millionaire he continues, like the Tjæreborg priest, to live in his village. But he has had Legoland built on a 2-acre site.

Centred on a charming model village designed in differing styles by a team of architects, who used 2 million Lego bricks to build it, Legoland includes also a superb doll museum, a Wild West riding centre, a children's road safety training course (which is great fun: you have to obey all the road signs correctly), and much else. A million people visited Legoland in its first 8 months, though the model village seems to interest old age pensioners more than children.

Legoland

Bornholm island

Nearly 200 km eastward journey by boat from Copenhagen, Bornholm lies within sight of southern Sweden. Its landscapes of tall granite cliffs and rocky coasts, sloping down to miles of silvery sand at Dueodde in the south, is as untypical of Denmark as anything could be. But its inhabitants have more than once shown themselves passionately Danish in character and outlook.

Bornholm (accent on the second syllable) is famous for its strangely clear light, its delicious smoked herrings, its often wild scenery, its brightly coloured farmhouses and other old buildings, its 4 ancient circular churches (built for defence against Wendish pirates, like two others in Denmark and a number in southern Sweden), and its minute harbours that were once filled with fishing craft and are now extremely popular with Danish and other yachtsmen. Bornholm is one of Denmark's main holiday areas.

The very comfortable and surprisingly cheap ferries from Copenhagen deposit you in Rønne, the capital and chief port, after a 7-hour journey (nightly all year, daily also in summer). You can also fly there in half an hour.

Rønne has whole streets of colourful small houses near the Store Torv (Great Market), its old town centre. On the island's east coast the harbour towns of Neksø, Svaneke, Tejn and, in particular, Gudhjem all have clusters of centuries-old small timbered houses. Bright colourings are traditional, with sandstone red and black predominating, but greens, yellows, blues and every imaginable hue are also now popular. Tejn is noteworthy as being the smallest of all the harbours.

Bornholm's scenery is at its wildest at Hammeren (The Hammer) at its northern tip. The cliffs here rise 250 feet above the sea. Surrounded by heather-covered slopes, which offer very pleasant walking, the gaunt ruins of Hammershus, a 13th-century fortress, look out towards Sweden. There are craggy cliffs at Helligdommen, north of Gudhjem on the eastern coast, and at Jons Kapel (John's Chapel: named after a hermit who used to preach there) south of Hammershus. Inland, the wooded Paradisbakkerne (Hills of Paradise), 3—5 km from the coast between Neksø and Svaneke, and the wooded, hilly Almindingen area at the island's centre are delightful to explore, especially on foot.

The four circular churches, originally defence towers, at Olsker (pronounced Oles-kor), Nyker (Nü-kor), Østerlars, and Nylars have each their own character. The church at Aakirkeby was also originally fortified and has a magnificently coloured and carved wooden pulpit.

Allinge and Sandvig, on the east coast just south of Hammeren, are the main holiday centres. But accommodation of every sort, including well-built chalets, is available in every part of the island. There are sandy beaches large and small scattered right round the coast—or you can dive into 10 or 20 feet of clear water from low rocks.

The island of Bornholm, 8 hours' voyage from Copenhagen

Ebeltoft

A market town since 1301 Ebeltoft still preserves its narrow, cobbled streets and a considerable number of small half-timbered, brightly coloured houses. One of them, built in 1576, used to be the Town Hall and is now a museum. The old Dyer's House (Farvegaarden) and Post House (Postgaarden) also house museum collections. Ebeltoft has a fine sandy beach in a well-sheltered bay on the further side of the Mols peninsula from Aarhus. With good hotels and other accommodation, including chalets, it is a holiday area very popular with Danes and others. The road distance from Aarhus is 47 km (30 miles). A fast, comfortable ferry, connecting Ebeltoft to Sjællands Odde (see North Zealand) in $1\frac{1}{2}$ hours with up to 18 sailings a day, provides a quick car route to Copenhagen and intermediate towns.

Esbjerg

Built to handle Danish exports to Britain just over a century ago, Esbjerg is the arrival port for comfortable and fast DFDS ferries from Harwich and Newcastle. Completely modern—only 20 people lived there in 1868—it is an extraordinarily clean and neat port. The town, too, is attractively laid out and has become increasingly industrial in recent years. Its attractions include a good municipal Art Gallery specialising in modern art and a seawater aquarium.

Esbjerg is the obvious starting-point for car tours of Denmark. It has good accommodation and restaurants. The ferry excursion to Fanø island (20 minutes: see separate entry), and perhaps a visit to the 200-mile sandy beach that starts immediately north, are well worth while.

Faaborg

Faaborg is a pleasant small port and yachting centre 40 km (25 miles) south of Odense. A number of attractive narrow streets and mainly 18th-century small timbered houses have survived, and there is a small art gallery devoted to the works of painters born on Funen island. Ferries operate from Faaborg to the tiny Danish islands of Avernakø and Lyø ($\frac{1}{2}$ hour), to Gelting in Germany ($2\frac{1}{4}$ hours), and to Søby near Ærø's western tip (1 hour). From Bøjden, 12 km west of Faaborg, you can cross to Fynshav on Als island (see Sønderborg), connected by a bridge to southern Jutland.

Faaborg, on the island of Funen

Falster island

Falster has Zealand and Møn to its north, Lolland on its west. Coming from Copenhagen you cross from Vordingborg on Zealand to the island's north coast by the vast Storstrøm road and rail bridge (Storstrømbroen), only 22 yards short of 2 miles, built by a British firm in 1937. From Lolland separate road and rail bridges cross the narrow Guldborg Sound separating the islands.

Falster's main towns are Stubbekøbing and Nykøbing (Nykøbing Falster to distinguish it from other Nykøbings). Falster is mainly flat, but has pleasant scenery round much of its coast, with a really magnificent long sandy beach down the eastern side of its southern tip. The beach takes its name from the minute village of Bøtø By (Bøtø Town). Europe's cheapest car ferry, run by Danish Railways, operates from Gedser, at Falster's southernmost point, to Warnemünde in East Germany: a car up to 6 m (19 ft 6 ins) and driver costs only 69 kr return (about £4.50) for the 2-hour journey. Another ferry connects Gedser to Travemünde in West Germany (3 hours).

Fanø island

Some 15 km long, lying off the west Jutland coast opposite Esbjerg, Fanø has long been a popular bathing and holiday resort. Its main attraction is the vast sandy beach down its western edge, wide enough to serve also as a summer road, complete with speed limit signs. The ferry from Esbjerg (20 minutes: departures every half-hour) lands visitors at Nordby village. Sønderho in the south has a number of old houses, including an attractive old inn, dating from sailing ship days, when Sønderho and Fanø were important shipping centres. 'Family'-standard hotels and chalet and campsite accommodation are available.

Fredericia

You pronounce the town's name Frederitsia or Fredereechia according to what part of Denmark you come from. Roughly 100 km from Esbjerg and 55 from Odense, Fredericia was built on a peninsula in 1650 by Frederik III (hence its name) to guard the Little Belt (Lille Bælt) strait between Jutland and Funen. The earth rampart hastily thrown up by thousands of Jutland peasants on the landward side is still almost intact. The streets were laid out in grid pattern to enable cannon on the ramparts to fire also at attackers landing on the shore.

Good bathing is possible at Snoghøj just south of the town. Hotels become specially full in early August, during Fredericia's annual Trade Fair.

Funen (Fyn) island

Funen (Fyn in Danish) is the large island centrally placed between Jutland and Zealand. It is connected to Jutland by the Little Belt bridge, to Zealand by rail and car ferries across the Great Belt, to Taasinge and Langeland islands by bridges, and to Germany, and Als and other smaller islands by ferries from Assens (in the west), Bøjden, Faaborg, and Svendborg.

Funen's capital, Odense, and the main centres of Faaborg, Nyborg, and Svendborg are described separately. To Danes Funen is 'the Garden of Denmark'—justifiably so, since flowers abound. The Svanninge Hills in the south, inland from Faaborg and Svendborg, are jokingly called 'the Funen Alps'. Though not very high, their wooded slopes provide lovely views and attractive walks and cycle rides. North-east of Odense (about 18 km) a special museum has been built at Ladby to house the famous Viking burial-ship excavated there in 1935 (follow the signs saying 'Ladby Skibet'). The chieftain buried in it 1000 years ago took with him to Valhalla his arms and armour, 4 hunting dogs, and 11 horses. At Nørre Lyndelse (about 15 km south of Odense) you can see the village musician's home where the great Danish composer Carl Nielsen (1865-1931) was born.

But perhaps the greatest of all Funen's glories is its many fine manor houses, concentrated most thickly in the island's south and west but found everywhere. The most notable of them, Egeskov (near Kværndrup, some 32 km south of Odense), is a superb Renaissance moated castle, surrounded by its original moat and by five gardens in different styles, including a reconstruction of the one laid out when the great house built.

Egeskov has a direct connection with Shakespeare's *Hamlet* that the 'castle at Elsinore' (see Helsingør) lacks. In 1599 an unmarried daughter of the house, Rigborg Brockenhuus, was found to be pregnant and was sentenced by the king to be imprisoned in her room in Egeskov for the rest of her father's life—happily he lived only 5 more years. The father of the illegitimate child was Frederik Rosenkrantz, recently returned with his friend Guldenstjerne (which is how old Danish records spell the name) from service with the Danish ambassador at the court of St James's, where he must surely have become known to Shakespeare.

Egeskov is outstanding by any standards. But the other manor houses are all worth seeing. Some are open to the public at certain times: others, like Egeskov, open only their gardens, and some can only be glimpsed from the road. The Odense Tourist Office can provide detailed and up-to-date information. We cannot unfortunately list details, but their names are:

Egeskov

Ulriksholm, Gyldensten, Margaard, Langesø (north of Odense), Juulskov, Holckenhavn, Ravnholt, Orbæklunde, Lykkesholm, Glorup, Hesselagergaard, Hvidkilde, Rygaard, Nakkebølle, Broholm, Mulerup, Holstenhus, Brahetrolleborg, Brahesborg, and Arreskov (to the south).

Charming old manor houses can be found all over Denmark, but Funen's are conveniently thickly clustered.

Grenaa

Now 3 km from the sea the pleasant old town of Grenaa was once a busy port at the mouth of the Green River (Gren Aa) on the Djurs peninsula projecting east into the Kattegat at Jutland's widest point. Randers lies 55 km west and Viborg 96. Ferries connect Grenaa's new harbour with Hundested on Zealand and with Anholt island in the middle of the Kattegat.

Haderslev

Haderslev straddles a narrow, winding fjord on Jutland's hilly east side, 24 km north of Aabenraa and 46 from the German frontier by highway A10. The chief points of interest are the mainly 15th-century Gothic Cathedral and the 'Latin School' founded in 1567 beside it. Accommodation is available.

Helsingør (Elsinore)

Since the 12th century there has been a castle at Helsingør, barely 4 km from the Swedish coast on the Øresund's other side. For over 400 years, up to 1857, the Danish kings acquired a fair proportion of their income by levying charges on shipping passing through the strait: the North European maritime nations bought them out with a down payment of £4 million. When Shakespeare wrote *Hamlet* English seamen were thoroughly familiar with Helsingør, which they called Elsinore, but Kronborg castle there never had any direct connection with Hamlet, who was a Prince of Jutland.

Kronborg in its present imposing form was built by Dutch architects for Frederik II in 1547, and rebuilt with alterations by Christian IV after a disastrous fire in 1629. You enter through a gate in the formidable outer ramparts and cross part of the old moat by a bridge. Rooms open to the public include the Guardroom; the State Apartments (including rooms first furnished

Kronborg Castle in Elsinore

for James VI of Scotland, later James I of England, after his marriage to Anne of Denmark in 1589); Christian IV's dining room containing 7 of the original tapestries representing Danish kings, woven at Helsingør by Flemish weavers in 1584; the Chapel which, unlike everything mentioned above, has retained its original appearance instead of the altered image provided by Christian IV; the Telegraph Tower, which provides a good view of the Sound and the Swedish coast; and the kitchens and casements, where you will see a statue of the mythical Holger Danske (Ogier the Dane), a sort of King Arthur figure who will reputedly waken and come to Denmark's aid if ever the country is in desperate straits.

The former Carmelite Monastery (Karmeliterklostret) off Havnegade just inland from the castle has survived in its original Gothic style. You can visit the refectory, chapter house, and chapel. The great organ composer Buxtehude, probably born at Hälsingborg on the Sound's Swedish side, was organist at the monastery from 1660 to 1667. The 16th-17th century English lutenist John Dowland dated some of his compositions from Helsingør.

Helsingør is also famous for its International People's College, founded in 1921 to promote international understanding.

Copenhagen is about 50 km away. Frequent ferries cross to Hälsingborg in 20 or 25 minutes.

Herning

Once a village known for its handweaving, Herning is now a sizeable and flourishing modern textile centre whose factories are known for imaginative modern ideas. The Angli factory, in particular, is almost as much art gallery as workplace, so that machine minders and office staff alike enjoy beautiful and frequently changed art displays while they work.

Herning holds a Textile Fair every March. It has a pleasant small museum of local life and history.

Herning lies 35 km west of Silkeborg by road and 77 km from Aarhus.

Holstebro

The little town of Holstebro (population 33,000) is an important west Jutland communications centre. Though ancient, its old buildings have all been destroyed by disastrous fires. And though small it is a town where all the arts—theatre, music, sculpture and everything else—flourish to an extraordinary degree. Leading orchestras and theatre companies visit the town. A large proportion of its inhabitants play musical instruments. And the Town Council spends the equivalent of about £5 a head each year on supporting these activities. It lies 51 km west of Viborg and 34 north-west of Herning.

Horsens

A sizeable industrial town situated on one of east Jutland's less attractive fjords, 51 km south of Aarhus and 27 north of Vejle by highway A10. Horsens was founded some 900 years ago and was an important fortified town in medieval times. A number of old buildings have survived. The pleasant 18th-century manor house Bygholm Slot, just west of the town, is now a hotel. The church in the little village of Ut (or Uth), about 6 km south-east of the town, has tombs of both the Rosenkrantz and Guldenstjerne families from which Shakespeare's *Hamlet* characters are drawn.

Jelling

A thousand years ago the little village of Jelling was Denmark's Viking capital. Two huge round barrows north and south of the ancient little church have always been regarded as the tombs of King Gorm the Old, first ruler of a united Denmark, and of his Queen, Thyra, the last Danish monarchs to be buried as pagans. Excavations, however, have shown that Gorm's Hill (Gorms Høj), south of the church, contained no burial chamber, while Thyra's Hill once held two bodies—we cannot tell whose.

Two large runic stones found at Jelling and now in the churchyard have been nicknamed 'Denmark's birth certificate' and 'Denmark's first court circular'. The larger, about 8 feet high, makes the first unmistakeable historical reference to Denmark. It was set up in memory of Gorm and Thyra by their son, Harald Bluetooth (Harald Blaatand), 'who won all Denmark and Norway for himself and made the Danes Christians'. It is remarkable for its carving of the crucified Christ embracing the world—Scandinavia's oldest representation of Christ—and for the fact that the runes run horizontally and not vertically, perhaps because the carver came from England. The smaller stone, about 5 feet high, tells us that 'King Gorm raised this monument to the memory of his wife Thyra'.

The little church has several remarkable features. The present building dates in part from the 10th or 11th centuries. But postholes for an earlier wooden church were discovered in 1948—you can see them through plate-glass let into the chancel floor. Specialists are certain that the large stone slab in the chancel, used 900 years ago as the altar, came—somehow—from Greece. Byzantine-style murals were discovered under the chancel's whitewash in 1874. And the church itself is centrally placed in a V of standing stones, almost certainly supplanting an earlier point of pagan worship.

Jelling lies about 14 km north-west of Vejle by the A18 and a kilometre or two more if you travel via the attractively hilly and well wooded Grejs valley *(Grejsdal)*.

Køge

Of all Zealand's old towns Køge alone has retained a really impressive number of old half-timbered houses, mostly from the 16th and 17th centuries. Since it also has two good beaches barely 40 km south of Copenhagen it is naturally a very popular holiday and excursion spot. It is also quite an important manufacturing town.

One of the town's main sights is the Nicolaj Kirke. Its huge fortified tower dates back to the 14th century. Any Wendish pirates who were caught used to be hanged from the tower windows. Hans

Køge

49

Andersen refers to them by their old name of 'Køge chickens'. The decorated pew ends, pulpit, and altarpiece date from the early 17th century. No. 20 Kirkestræde (Church Street), which leads from St Nicholas' to Torvet (The Market) is reputedly Denmark's oldest house of known date (1527), and other old houses can be seen in streets leading off Torvet. The Town Hall (Raadhus) in Nørregade (North Street) was built in the 16th century but given a new façade in 1803. Another old house in Nørregade houses the Køge Museum. There is of course a main tourist office in Køge.

Køge is a good base from which to explore Stevns, the broad peninsula ending in cliffs, known as Stevns Klint, over 30 m (100 feet) high and 15 km long, between Køge Bay (Køge Bugt) and Fakse Bay. There is good bathing and good scenery in this region.

Kolding

Kolding is another of hilly east Jutland's attractively situated fjord towns. It stands at the point where the A1 Esbjerg-Odense-Copenhagen road crosses the A10 from the German frontier to northern Jutland, some 63 km east of Esbjerg and 70 km west of Odense. Originally a fortress town, it now manufactures textiles, hardware, bacon, chocolate, and much else.

Of the town's old buildings the most important is the Koldinghus, the royal castle built in 1248 to ward off incursions from the south (the present German frontier is 70 km away). Burnt down by an accidental fire in 1808, during the Napoleonic Wars, it has never since been rebuilt, but its ruins provide the town with a picturesque backdrop.

Korsør

Though relatively important as a Zealand manufacturing town some 110 km west of Copenhagen, Korsør is known to visitors mainly as a terminus for the train ferries crossing the Great Belt. The car ferries, nowadays much busier, ply from Halsskov immediately north. Advance car bookings are essential in summer.

Krusaa

This small south Jutland village is the frontier crossing point of the main A10-E3 highway from Germany.

Læsø island

This once-remote island in the Kattegat is famous for its heath-and-dune scenery, its old timbered houses thatched with sea-grass, its pines and birchwoods, and its fine bathing. You reach it by ferry in 1 hour 40 mins from Frederikshavn (see North Jutland).

Langeland island

Langeland, some 55 km long and 10 km at its widest, lies south-west of Funen. You can reach it by road from Svendborg, across bridges connecting Funen to Taasinge island, Taasinge to tiny Siø island, and Siø to Rudkøbing, Langeland's main town. Rudkøbing is also connected to Marstal (see Ærø island) by ferry (1 hour). Lohals, near Langeland's northern tip, has a ferry connection to Korsør (1½ hours). From Spodsberg on the island's eastern side you can reach Nakskov on Lolland island in 1 hour 20 mins. From Bagenkop at the southern tip, ferries ply to Kiel in West Germany in 2 hours 20 mins (up to 3 departures daily in summer).

Rudkøbing is an old port and has been a market town since 1287. Many timbered houses have survived, and its church dates from the 12th century. The town's Langeland Museum has a first-rate collection illustrating the island's history.

In the rest of the island the small settlements are not particularly important. But the scenery is pleasantly hilly and dotted with windmills, for which Langeland is famous, and there are cliffs at Ristinge in the south. The fine moated manor house of Tranekær, about 12 km north of Rudkøbing, has been a royal residence since 1231. There are lesser manors at Stensgaard, Nedergaard, and Egeløkke in the north, and Skovsgaard, Hjortholm, and Broløkke in the south.

There are good bathing beaches at Ristinge and Østerbadet in the south, and at Spodsbjerg, Lohals, and Emmerbølle (near Tranekær, on the west coast). A main tourist office operates at Rudkøbing.

Lolland island

As its name 'Lowland' suggests, most of Lolland is really flat. But there are some attractive corners—notably the manor houses of Søholm (overlooking the large lake south of Maribo), Knuthenborg and its lovely 'English' park about 6 km north of Maribo, and Kristianssæde, about 12 km south-west. Apart from Maribo the main towns are Sakskøbing and Nakskov.

A special sort of attraction, in the form of a really superb veteran car museum, is provided by Aalholm Castle, itself an attractive old manor house near Nysted on the island's south coast, about 30 km from both Maribo and Rødbyhavn. Nysted has a fine beach to its east.

Lolland lies between Langeland and Falster islands. It is connected to the former by the Nakskov-Spodsbjerg ferry (1 hour 20 mins) and to the latter by bridges across the narrow strait. The ferry that comes into the little modern port of Rødbyhavn, on Lolland's south

coast, from Puttgarden in West Germany constitutes a major car
route into Denmark (crossing 1 hour: up to 28 departures daily in
summer).

Møn island

Møn's main feature is the magnificent stretch of high chalk cliffs,
known as Møns Klint, at its eastern edge. Running for a good 8 km
their maximum height is 128 m (about 425 feet). Many of the
formations have been eroded into strange shapes, given fanciful
names like 'Queen's Chair' and 'Summer Spire'. They are shot with
varying colours, covered for much of their extent with massive
beechwoods, and cut by ravines which you can clamber down to
reach the beach. Lower cliffs continue northwards. Ulvshale, north
of Stege, Møn's 'capital', offers good bathing, and churches at
Elmelunde, Keldby, and Fanefjord contain very striking 15th-
century frescoes of country scenes. Møn is linked to Zealand by a
road bridge.

Møn's Cliffs—one of Denmark's outstanding beauty spots

Mors island and the Limfjord

An inland island in a country made up mostly of islands seems odd. But Mors lies in the middle of the vast and complicated expanse of water, known as the Limfjord, which cuts right across northern Jutland. On its western side it is protected against North Sea flooding by dykes. In the east it provides Aalborg, seemingly inland, with a deep-sea harbour.

Nykøbing (called Nykøbing Mors to distinguish it from towns of the same name on Falster and Zealand islands) is Mors's only town. It is famous chiefly for its oyster beds. A thousand and more years ago the surrounding Limfjord's shores provided raiding bases for Vikings. Today, a number of towns stand round it. The most important are: Skive, Struer, Lemvig, Thisted (or Tisted), and Løgstør.

Skive is a charming town, beautifully located on a hill sloping down to the Skive Fjord, an inner inlet off the Limfjord. It is an extremely popular yachting centre. Though very ancient the church is almost its only surviving old building. Struer is a purely modern industrial town, but Lemvig is another ancient settlement with a natural harbour. Løgstør, now a market town, was once important for its herring fisheries. Thisted, main town of the narrow strip of land separating the Limfjord from the North Sea, is the chief settlement of the region called Thy (pronounced Tü).

North Jutland and the North-West Coast

From Esbjerg northwards, Jutland's entire west coast with its magnificent wide sandy beach backed by extensive dunes, occasional cliffs, and sometimes vast lagoons, is a sort of continuous holiday area in summer. There are relatively few towns apart from the lovely old settlement of Ringkøbing, on the landward side of the large Ringkøbing Fjord lagoon, a number on the shores of the extensive and complex Limfjord (see Mors and the Limfjord), and others near Jutland's northern tip. Even the villages—Nørre Vorupor, Klitmøller, Slettestrand, Svinkløv, Hanstholm (noted for its cliffs), Bulbjerg (also with cliffs), Torupstrand, and the rest are tiny—until you come to the larger and livelier resort centres of Blokhus and Løkken, with smaller Lønstrup beyond. Apart from 1st-class hotels at Hanstholm, Blokhus, and Løkken the main pattern of holidaymaking is one of family stays in more modest hotel and pensions, in chalets, and on campsites, with the beach and nature as holidaymakers' main delights: there are bird sanctuaries among the lagoons.

Hirtshals and Frederikshavn near Jutland's northern tip are port towns with ferries operating respectively to Kristiansand (4 hours) and Arendal (4 hours: both in Norway); and to Larvik in Norway (5 hours) and Oslo (10 hours, summer only). Hjørring, inland, is a market town noted for its parks. There are good bathing beaches north of Frederikshavn and close to Bangsbo, an 18th-century manor that is now a museum, about 2 km south. On the way north to Skagen you can make a detour about 12 km short of the town to the dunes of Raabjerg Mile, which have been moving slowly eastwards for years.

The town of Skagen, busy fishing port, summer resort, and artists' centre all in one, rather like St Ives in Cornwall, is however the main attraction for visitors in this corner of Denmark. It has restaurants, a number of small hotels, and a small museum of the type you expect in every self-respecting Danish town. Skagen's is housed in old fishermen's cottages and deals largely with the region's seafaring history.

Skagen has been transformed in English into The Skaw. But the English name is mostly applied to the sandy spit of land which forms Jutland's northern extremity, known in Danish as Grenen (The Tip). It is a very unimpressive headland—except that it enables you to stand with one foot in the North Sea and the other in the Kattegat.

North Zealand

Most of the northern part of Zealand (Sjælland) island is outstandingly popular as a holiday resort, not only because it is close to Copenhagen but also because it offers outstandingly pleasant and—off the main roads between Copenhagen and Helsingør—peaceful countryside, a wide choice of hotels and other accommodation, and excellent bathing from large sandy beaches in the extreme north. (The fastest route between Copenhagen and Helsingør is the crowded motorway.)

The coast is built-up almost the whole 30 km from Klampenborg on Copenhagen's northern outskirts to Helsingør (see separate entries), and the road flanking it is mercilessly busy in summer. While the beaches are at best only a few yards wide bathing is by no means impossible, and there are a number of pleasant and comfortable places where you can stay, such as Snekkersten, about 4 km south of Helsingør. Humlebæk, about 5 km south of Snekkersten, boasts the superb Louisiana Museum of Modern Art, where concerts are also given and where you can eat very well in the museum's famous restaurant.

North of Helsingør Marienlyst has a pleasant beach and a famous luxury hotel. Hellebæk, about 5 km further on, can boast an even better beach and another luxury hotel. Hornbæk, 12 km from Helsingør, is a fishing village with old streets and houses lying below wooded hills with magnificent views across the Sound.

As you continue round Zealand's northernmost tip you come to a series of ever better and larger beaches at Dronningmølle, Gilleleje (another old fishing village), Raageleje, Tisvildeleje, and Liseleje, almost 50 km from Helsingør (*leje* means 'fishing village'). Numerous small chalets, mostly modest hotels, and campsites are the main accommodation in this popular region.

From all round this coast roads lead inland to the delightfully peaceful town of Hillerød, centred on the royal castle of Frederiksborg. The builder-king Christian IV designed and built the present castle, after pulling down the older one where he had been born. The National Historical Museum, administered by the Carlsberg Trust, is housed in the castle. Lovely Grib Skov Wood stretches north for some 10 km from Hillerød, with the lake called Esrum Sø east of it. Another fine royal castle, named Fredensborg (Peace Castle: so called because peace was signed here between Denmark and Sweden in 1620) stands on the lake's further side.

If you continue round Zealand's coast from Liseleje you come by criss-cross roads to the steel-and-explosives town of Frederiksværk, the little herring-fishing town of Nykøbing (Nykøbing Sjællands to distinguish it from its namesakes), the industrial and port town of Holbæk, and ancient Kalundborg, once a major royal stronghold but now known for its manufactures.

Along Zealand's north-west coast ferries operate from Hundested (near Frederiksværk) to Grenaa in Jutland (2½ hours), from Sjællands Odde to Ebeltoft (1½ hours), and from Kalundborg to Samsø island (2 hours), Aarhus (3 hours), and Juelsminde (see Vejle: 2½ hours).

About half way between Nykøbing and Kalundborg, in Faarevejle village church, you can see the Earl of Bothwell, husband of Mary Queen of Scots. Imprisoned for the last 11 years of his life, he was chained to a pillar in the dungeons of Dragsholm Castle, not far from Faarevejle, for the last 5. Mummified by some freak accident his body is still kept in a glass-topped coffin.

Nyborg

Nyborg, on Funen's eastern side and 30 km from Odense, is one end of the Great Belt train-ferry crossing: motorists embarking and disembarking at Knudshoved by-pass it completely. Yet a very pleasant small town lies behind the tangle of railway lines and the busy motorway, with excellent bathing and several hotels, including one of Denmark's best, just north of the town.

Its main point of interest is its castle, of which only one carefully and lovingly restored wing remains out of the original 4.

Scandinavia's oldest royal castle, it was built in 1170 to close the Great Belt to marauding Wendish pirates. From 1282 until 1413 the country's first parliament, called the Danehof, met here. Three wings were destroyed by the Swedes in the war of 1658-60. Today, original geometrical wall-paintings have been uncovered, the royal family has lent furniture going back to the 15th century, and long untended beams and woodwork have been beautifully restored, so that you get a very vivid idea of the castle's appearance in its heyday. Nyborg's church was dedicated by Queen Margrethe in 1388. The Crusaders' House (Korsbrødregaarden) stands close to it. Founded as a monastery in 1396 it was taken over by the Knights Templar in 1441.

Odense

Odense (pronounced roughly like Aw-thencer—though no Dane expects a foreigner to know this) is the capital of Funen island, Denmark's third largest city, an important port as well as industrial centre, and—Hans Andersen's birthplace. This last fact bulks so large in most travellers' minds that they hardly ever leave themselves time to discover how pleasant and attractive Odense is.

The city's most staggering modern building is its Town Hall, built in clear rivalry with those of Copenhagen and Aarhus and completed only in 1955. The original one (1880) was unusual enough in having as frontage a facsimile of Siena's ancient Palazzo Pubblico. The new structure retains this façade, while providing a lot of extra accommodation of often revolutionary design and almost unimaginable sumptuousness. Every visible thing except light bulbs and window glass was specially designed. Groups are taken round at fixed hours.

Odense's oldest building, the Cathedral of Sankt Knud (St Canute, not the king we remember but Canute II, 1080-1086), faces the Town Hall across the square. It dates from the 13th century and experts say it is Denmark's finest Gothic church. Like virtually all Danish churches it is brick-built and light and colourful, with a particularly remarkable altarpiece consisting of 300 detachable figures.

St Canute himself—or rather his bones—can be seen in a glass-covered coffin in the crypt. The skull fracture caused by a stone thrown when the mob broke into St Alban's Church in Odense is easily visible. (The old St Alban's disappeared long ago, though there is a modern Albani Kirke.) Canute's shrine was one of two which medieval pilgrims visited. It is possible that the other was occupied by the body of the English monk St Alban. Two 16th-century Danish kings and their queens are also buried in the Cathedral.

Remains of a Benedictine monastery similarly dedicated to St Canute adjoin the Cathedral, with a well kept monastic-style herb garden beside them. Another garden, just beyond the monastery's, is a memorial to Hans Andersen. The River Odense (Odense Aa) flows through it.

No. 3 Munkemøllestræde, where Hans Andersen (always referred to as H.C. Andersen in Danish) lived from the age of 2 till he was 14, is preserved as a museum. It consists of one room and a kitchen. The most important collection of items connected with him is, however, H.C. Andersens Hus (Hans Andersen's House) on the corner of Hans Jensensstraede and Bangs Boder. It incorporates his birthplace. You will find assembled here, apart from copies of his works in 70 or more languages, things which he used, including the rope he always carried in case a hotel where he was staying caught fire, and specimens of his superb cut-out paper designs.

A motor boat trip along the very attractive River Odense, from Munke Mose park to the Zoo and Tivoli amusement gardens (based on Copenhagen's) and on to the Funen Village open-air museum, makes a very pleasant excursion. The Funen Village (Den fynske Landsby) consists of typical old village homes, re-erected in the same way as at Copenhagen's Frilandsmuseum and Aarhus's Den gamle By. A special attraction is the Sortebrokro (Black Bridge Inn), a genuine old village hostelry, with modern kitchens attached which serves excellent food. Other possible excursion places are mentioned under Funen.

Odense has a varied selection of hotels and other accommodation, including a motel on the outskirts suitable for motor tourists, together with numerous restaurants and the collection of late-night spots you expect in any sizeable Danish town.

Randers

Randers is another of the many Danish towns with a long history, a pleasant layout, and numerous modern factories—whose products, in Randers' case, include bacon for a lot of British breakfasts. The 14th-century Sankt Mortens Kirke is perhaps the finest of the town's old buildings. The Town Hall dates from the 18th century, with what is reputedly Randers' oldest surviving building, the Paaskesønnernes Gaard, on its left. A narrow street beside this old house leads to surviving portions of a 15th-century monastery dedicated to the Holy Ghost and now called Helligaandshuset. In the late 18th and early 19th century these housed Randers' 'Latin school' (grammar school), several of whose pupils became famous in Denmark.

Randers lies roughly 40 km east of Viborg and 36 km north of Aarhus.

Rebild National Park and Rold Skov

In 1912 a group of Danish-born American citizens bought a piece of land in the Rebild Hills (Rebild Bakker) about 25 km south of Aalborg and gave it to the Danish Government on condition that a ceremony commemorating the American Declaration of Independence should be held there every July 4th. In 1934 a replica of Lincoln's log cabin was built with materials from each American state and furnished with exhibits illustrating the early pioneers' and Indians' life. Since World War II, in particular, the annual celebration has grown tremendously in importance.

Rold Skov, surrounding the National Park, is extensive enough today, but is only a tiny part of the vast forest which once covered Himmerland, the home—as some scholars think—of the ancient Cimbri tribe. The soil is sandy and dotted with clumps of beeches, though spruce is the commonest tree, and oaks, aspens, heather, rosemary, juniper, whortleberry, and bilberry also grow there. The landscape is decidedly hilly, and cut by deep ravines, with clear lakes in several places. You can enjoy wonderful walks here.

Inside the National Park area a number of buildings have been erected close to the log cabin. They include a restaurant, a Youth Hostel, and the Hjemstavn- og Spillemands Museum devoted to the wandering fiddlers *(spillemænd)* once common in this region, and to their instruments and way of life. A carved stone commemorates also the Cimbri who 'went out from this district 120 BC'.

Apart from the Youth Hostel, accommodation is available at the Rold Stor Kro, a modern hotel beside the A10 main road, in the village of Skørping east of Rold Skov; and in the small town of Hobro, 20 km south on the main road (see also Viking remains).

Ribe

Situated on marshy ground close to the sea in the southern part of the west Jutland coast some 50 km north of Tønder and the German frontier, Ribe is one of Denmark's most interesting towns. Though still small it was first mentioned in history in AD 862 and has been a bishopric since 948—which makes it Denmark's most ancient town. It boasts an outstandingly interesting Cathedral and a lot of old cobbled streets and little timber-frame houses, as well as a castle going back to the 12th century.

The Cathedral, dedicated to Our Lady (Vor Frue), was begun about 1130 and built with stone brought from the Rhineland. Much of the early architecture is Romanesque, but it includes a very unusual (for Europe) Byzantine dome over the nave-transept crossing. The large square tower, intended partly for defence, was first built about 1250 and rebuilt 400 years later. The smaller, south-west tower dates only from 1896, but replaces a medieval structure. Sculpture of almost every date from 1130 to the present decorates the interior, including several works by Anne Marie Carl-Nielsen, the famous composer's wife. The fine organ dates from 1635 and the highly decorative pulpit from 1597.

The fine 15th-century Town Hall stands in the heart of the old town. It was here in 1460 that King Christian I, after becoming Duke of Slesvig (Schleswig in German) and Count of Holstein (Holsten in Danish), issued his famous decree that the two should never be separated—and thus laid the foundation of the 'Schleswig-Holstein question' which bedevilled European politics throughout the 19th century and was only resolved by a plebiscite in 1920 in which North Slesvig opted to be Danish and South Schleswig and Holstein German.

Ribe used to be famous for the storks which came regularly each year to nest on the roofs of old houses. In recent years their numbers have fluctuated, though a few can usually be seen in summer.

Hotels and other accommodation are available in Ribe, including an excellent municipal campsite. The town has a main tourist office.

Ringsted

A capital city in Viking times and a favourite royal centre up to the reign of Christian IV (1588-1648), Ringsted is today a simple market town, notable mainly for its church of St Benedict (Sankt Bendt Kirke). Originally part of a Benedictine monastery founded about 1080, St Benedict's is Denmark's oldest brick-built church and the burial place of many Danish kings and queens of the 13th and 14th centuries. Queen Ingeborg's 14th-century tomb is covered by a brass similar in style to brasses of corresponding date in King's Lynn. Bjernede village, about 12 km west of Ringsted (turn off the A1 at Slaglille), has Zealand's only round church, built like those on Bornholm.

Ringsted lies about 30 km south-west of Roskilde and 60 km from Copenhagen by the A1.

Roskilde

In its early days Roskilde was Denmark's most important city. From 1020 till supplanted by Copenhagen in 1416 it was the seat of the Danish court. Its first church, made of wood, was built by Harald Bluetooth in about 960 and its first bishop, appointed 100 years later, was probably an Englishman. Absalon, founder of Copenhagen, became Bishop of Roskilde in 1157 when he was only 29

The city's political importance has declined today and it has become instead an important industrial centre. But its Cathedral, reputedly Denmark's finest, still draws tens of thousands of visitors every year. It contains the tombs of all but 3 of Denmark's kings from the last 500 years, and all but 4 of their queens. Margrethe, Queen of Denmark, Norway, and Sweden, who died in 1412, is also buried here.

The present lofty building, the third since Harald Bluetooth's little wooden church, was started in Romanesque style by Absalon and completed in Gothic a century later. The prominent green spires were added by the indefatigable Christian IV.

You enter through the south porch. Immediately on your right is the earliest of 4 Royal Chapels added to the original groundplan, that of Christian I, built in 1459. A single column supports the vaulted ceiling. The heights of several kings marked on it show a little light-hearted boasting. Christian I claims 7 ft 6 ins (against his real 6 ft 2 ins) and Peter the Great of Russia 6 ft 10 ins. Christian I, Christian III, and Frederik II and their queens are buried here.

Further along on the right steep steps lead to the ornate Frederik V's Chapel, containing the sarcophagi of Christian VI, Frederik V, Christian VII, Frederik VI, Christian VIII, and Frederik VII, who reigned, in that order, from 1730 to 1863.

On the nave's opposite side Christian IV's Chapel is separated from the main church by a lovely ironwork screen, dating from 1618. Christian IV and Frederik III, who between them reigned from 1588 to 1670, lie here. And in the last of the Chapels, added in 1923, are the sarcophagi of Christian IX, Frederik VIII, Christian X, and Frederik IX (1863-1973). Queen Margrethe, Christian V, and Frederik IV are buried behind the high altar.

Apart from its many royal tombs, most of them carved sarcophagi like those of the Danish kings of England in Winchester Cathedral, the church has a fine gilded wood altarpiece (1580), carved choir stalls (1420), a 16th-17th century organ, and an extraordinary 16th-century clock. Mechanical figures strike the hours and quarters; St George's clockwork horse rears up on every hour; and a clockwork dragon just as regularly lets out a piercing squeal.

Coach excursions from Copenhagen and many tours of Denmark include visits to Roskilde Cathedral.

Rømø island

Separated by 8 km of sea from the low-lying west Jutland coast midway between Ribe and Tønder, Rømø has become a popular holiday area in recent years. It has a magnificently wide sandy beach, backed by extensive dunes, facing the North Sea. The village of Havneby in the south has a modern fishing harbour and there is a museum of local history, the Kommandøgaard, on the island. A causeway links Rømø to the low-lying mainland opposite the little town of Skærbaek.

Samsø island

Samsø, midway between Jutland and north Zealand, has also become popular with holidaymakers in recent years. Apart from a number of good, but slightly pebbly, beaches the island is known for its varied landscapes, picturesque little towns, and numerous old farms. Mainly simple accommodation is available. Ferries operate from Aarhus (2 hours), Hov (east of Horsens in Jutland: $1\frac{1}{4}$ hours), and Kalundborg (2 hours).

Silkeborg, the Silkeborg Lakes, and Skanderborg

This region contains some of the best of Denmark's gentle scenery. It lies about 40 km west of Aarhus and is ideal not only for walking and cycling but also for canoe touring. All necessary gear can be hired from firms in and around Silkeborg at reasonable rates: full information is available from the Silkeborg main tourist office.

The whole region is wooded and intersected with paths, mostly well signposted. Hills surrounding the many lakes include mainland Denmark's highest point, 147 m (482 feet) above sea level, and laughingly named Himmelbjerget (The Sky Mountain). As all the lakes are connected by the River Guden (Guden Aa) and its tributaries, extensive canoe-camping trips are popular. Regular pleasure boat services also operate from Silkeborg to Svejbæk, Himmelbjerget, Laven, and Ry. The most entertaining of the vessels used is the paddle-steamer 'Hjelen', which made its first trip to Himmbjerget with King Frederik VII on board on June 24th, 1861 and has been in continuous service ever since.

A favourite short walk takes you downhill from Silkeborg's Town Square (Torvet) to the bridge over the Guden and then to the right, along the riverside track to the hotel at Hattenæs. If you continue further you can climb various hills on your left which provide good views. A still longer walk (about 15 km) takes you over the hills to the summit of the Sky Mountain, where there is a hotel and restaurant. There are many other possible trips.

Skanderborg, about 32 km south-east of Silkeborg and on the main A10 highway between Horsens and Aarhus, is another centre from which this region can be explored. In medieval times it was an important royal centre, and its position between two major lakes makes it popular with holidaymakers today.

Silkeborg Museum contains one of the most striking of all Denmark's museum exhibits—the so-called 'Tollund Man'. This is the almost perfectly preserved body of a man, buried in a peat bog about 8 km west of Silkeborg some 2000 years ago and discovered by accident in 1950, rather like the 'Grauballe Man' in Aarhus Museum (see Aarhus). It is often commented that the Tollund Man has the same facial characteristics as many modern Jutlanders.

Quick visits to the Silkeborg-Skanderborg region can be made by car, excursion coach, or public transport from Aarhus and other centres. Plenty of accommodation of most types is available in the area.

Sønderborg and Als island

Sønderborg is the chief town of Als island, immediately off the extreme southern end of Jutland's east coast. It is connected to the mainland by a bridge across the narrow strait. As part of North Slesvig Sønderborg was concerned in the Prussian wars of 1848-9 and 1864: Dybbøl Mill, where the Danes suffered a disastrous defeat in 1864, lies just across the strait.

In Sønderborg itself the main attractions are the castle, Physical Culture Folk High School, the extensive yacht harbour, and the ancient annual Tilting Festival (Ringrider Fest), held on the 2nd weekend of every July.

The castle stands on a point of land south-west of the town. It contains a delightful chapel, built in 1568-70, that was not only Denmark's first Lutheran church but also the country's first piece of building in Renaissance style. Other rooms are devoted mainly to a military museum of local history. The Folk High School was built in 1952 as Denmark's most modern sports training centre: parties are shown round in summer. The Tilting Festival centres on a competition in which riders aim a lance at a 2″ ring, as they have been doing for 400 years, and includes processions, football matches, wrestling, and general jollification going on till the early hours.

Sønderborg makes a pleasant base for excursions to places like Dubbøl Mill and the royal manor of Graasten some 13 km beyond it. Als island offers pleasant undulating countryside with attractive small villages and good bathing at such places as Høruphav, 3 km east of Sønderborg; the large Kegnæs peninsula south of Høruphav; Mommark, the old ferry terminal 23 km due east of Sønderborg; and Fynshav, the modern terminal to the north.

Svendborg

Roughly 48 km south of Odense on Funen's southern coast, Svendborg is one of Denmark's busiest and most important yachting centres. It is also a charming small town, with a number of old houses in its centre, and a lovely position overlooking the strait separating it from Taasinge island. As a touring base from which to visit southern Funen, with its hills, woods and numerous manor houses, and the islands of Ærø, Taasinge, and Langeland, it is almost ideal. There is good bathing close to the town and at other points nearby. As Svendborg is a very popular holiday base there is no shortage of accommodation of every type, nor of restaurants and entertainment.

One of the town's special attractions is the Zoological Museum, containing among other things examples of all Denmark's birds. St Nicholas' Church dates from the 13th century. A very pleasant walk leads eastward from the harbour along the shore to the area known as Christiansminde, where there are some good hotels. A somewhat antique ship makes excursions to the islands of Taasinge and adjacent Thurø, and a private collection of pipes from all over the world has been turned into a popular museum.

Taasinge and Thurø islands

Connected to Svendborg by a high bridge crossing Svendborg Sound, Taasinge is a very colourful little island. Its main town, Troense, boasts a number of old houses, a school that dates from 1654, and a good little private museum devoted to the days of sailing ships, housed in the old schoolhouse. Valdemar's Castle (actually a rebuilt manor house dating from the 17th century) overlooks the sea south of tiny Troense. A large oak close to it is said to be 800 years old. From the top of Bregninge's church tower in the middle of the island you can see half south Funen and the German coast near Flensburg on a clear day. The church itself has a colourful pulpit (1621), gaily decorated pew ends, and several of the model ships normal in all Danish seafaring-area churches. Tiny Thurø, connected to Funen east of Svendborg by a road bridge, offers good bathing as well as places to stay at.

Tønder and surroundings

Once an important port but now several miles from the sea, Tønder was founded in the 13th century. Today it is famous for its lace and is a very colourful little town. Several 17th-century houses have survived, including the Town Hall, a 'Latin School' (grammar school), and an old apothecary's shop. The red roof and tall spire of Christ Church (1592, incorporating parts of an older building) are visible for miles across the low-lying flat land surrounding the town, and the church's interior is extraordinarily decorated. The town museum contains a good collection of furniture, ceramics, and other items.

Møgeltønder, 5 km west of Tønder on the road to Højer and the sea, is an extremely attractive village of thatched cottages. Løgumkloster, 16 km north, off the A11 road to Ribe, is all that remains of a large Cistercian abbey founded in the 11th or 12th century. The Gothic church, library, sacristy, and vaulted chapter house have survived and can be visited. The marshy countryside round about gives a clear idea of the reclamation work necessary before the land could be made productive.

Vejle and its fjord

Although Vejle is a relatively important manufacturing town it is also, thanks mainly to the lovely, hilly east Jutland fjord on which it stands, one of Denmark's most popular holiday centres. Roughly 30 km north of Kolding on the main A10 the town is hilly enough to be called 'Denmark's Mountain Town'. You can certainly ski there if the snow is thick enough in winter. The town is plentifully supplied with hotels and other accommodation and is famous for the number and quality of its nightspots. It is conveniently close to Jelling and other places of interest.

Vejle's main attraction however is the fjord at whose head it lies. Of all the bays cutting sharply into Jutland's hilly east coast this is undoubtedly the most attractive, combining wooded slopes with a curving shape and pleasant bathing beaches, near all of which you will find good hotels and restaurants.

Vejle's main bathing beach, Albuen, lies on the fjord's north shore. You can bathe also at Tirsbaek, Fakkegrav, and Juelsminde (where the ferries from Kalundborg arrive) on that side of the bay. On the south side Munkebjerg and Hvidbjerg are the best spots. Munkebjerg has a well-known hotel and restaurant on top of its wooded slopes.

Viborg

Viborg is one of Jutland's most ancient and historic towns. Its name comes from the 'Sacred Hill' *(Vi Bjerg)* where pagan gods were once worshipped and where the Cathedral now stands. Kings were elected by chieftains assembled here in ancient times. Here, too, Denmark's first coins were struck during the reign of Canute the Great (1018-1035).

Unfortunately, because of repeated fires, few of the town's buildings go back beyond the 18th century. Viborg was created a bishopric in 1065 and the building of a Cathedral began in 1130 with granite brought all the way from Central Germany. Fires and restoration have left nothing of the old building, but the reconstructed version is still Europe's largest granite church, with towers over 40 m high that are a landmark for miles around. Opposite the Cathedral's west front the Old Town Hall, built in 1728, is now a museum. There are a number of other old houses in Sankt Mogensgade near the Cathedral.

Viborg lies about 80 km south of Aalborg by the A13, and 26 north of Silkeborg. It is a useful base for excursions—to the wooded Dollerup Hills some 8 km south, to Skive on the Limfjord, to Silkeborg, and to the lovely scenery and excellent open-air museum of Hjerl Hede, almost equidistant from Viborg, Skive, and Holstebro. Similar in type to Copenhagen's Frilandsmuseum, Aarhus's Den gamle By, and Odense's Den fynske Landsby, the museum has the advantage of being set in scenery that typifies the sort of countryside from which its houses come. It is also remarkable in being a completely private undertaking.

Viking remains

Apart from the Lindholm Høj graveyard at Nørresundby (see Aalborg) and the Ladby Ship (see Funen), there are important Viking forts at Trelleborg on Zealand (off the A1 about 12-13 km east of Korsør or Halsskov) and at Fyrkat about 4 km south-west

Excavations at Lindholm Høje

65

of Hobro in Jutland (see Rebild National Park). Though Trelleborg is the more elaborate, both follow the same general plan of an encircling rampart enclosing a number of building groups designed with mathematical precision. Both fortresses can be dated to roughly AD 990, and it is not impossible that they were constructed by Sweyn Forkbeard shortly before his invasion of England.

There are of course numerous Viking relics in Copenhagen's National Museum and in other museums throughout Denmark. But there is one other major outdoor trace of the Vikings worth hunting out. This is the 'Viking Road', known also as the 'Ox Road' because cattle being exported to Germany were driven down it 150 years ago. Running south from Viborg, its first 80 km coincide with the Viborg-Vejle highway, A13. After that it branches off down Jutland's west side. Parts are used today for riding holidays. Local tourist offices will help you find it.

Greenland and the Faroe Islands

These are parts of Denmark too! Greenland (2 million sq. km.) is the world's largest island after Australia. Although it is as icy as Iceland is green the ice-free 14% of it is as large as England and Wales together—but inhabited by only about 45,000 Eskimos and 7,000 Danish settlers. Regular air services operate to Greenland from Copenhagen and Reykjavik, and there is an infrequent and variable steamer route from Copenhagen. Major settlements have either good modern hotels or acceptable guesthouses. More and more firms are organising group tours, many of which include things like fishing, shooting, rock-climbing, sledge tours, and botany, zoology, or geology. Prices are decidedly not cheap. English is spoken only by some Danish settlers, and steamer and helicopter services inside the country are apt to involve delays measured in days rather than hours.

The Faroes—the name means 'sheep islands'—are more easily accessible, though still remote enough to have retained many medieval customs. They consist of 18 islands which provide superb scenery and excellent walking, trout fishing, and birdwatching. Though roads are good (you can take your own car or hire one) other communications are uncertain because of the weather. Sound accommodation is available. You reach the Faroes by regular air services from Kirkwall (Shetland Islands), Bergen (Norway), Reykjavik (Iceland), and Copenhagen; or by sea from Esbjerg, Leith (Scotland), or Copenhagen. English is widely spoken, but prices, again, are not low. Information for both Greenland and the Faroes is available from the Danish National Tourist Office (address p 18), and for the Faroes direct from: Føroya Ferdamannafelag, DK-3800 Torshavn.

Life Danish Style

Land and People

Denmark is an unusual country. It consists of Jutland, a large peninsula joined to northern Germany, and some 483 islands, about 100 of which are inhabited. Stretching roughly 320 km (200 miles) from north to south and with an average breadth of about 180 km (100 miles), Jutland is attached to the European mainland by a neck of land barely 45 km (under 30 miles) wide. Denmark's largest island, Zealand (or Sealand: Sjælland in Danish), extends for roughly 90 by 60 miles. One result of this unusual land configuration is that virtually no part of Denmark lies more than 30 miles from the sea which, to Danes, is almost as much part of their heritage as the land they live on.

Denmark is not a naturally fertile country—it has only been made productive by a great deal of hard work which began with the foundation of the Danish Heath Society (Det Danske Hedeselskab) in 1866. Most of the land consists simply of debris deposited by melting glaciers at the end of the world's last Ice Age.

While Denmark's countryside is unlike anything else in Europe, her population is even more unusual—and unusually likeable. The modern Danes' ancestors moved northward into their country some 10,000 years ago, since when there has been no major admixture of foreign blood through conquest and invasion or immigration. When a man's accidentally mummified body was discovered in a Jutland bog some years ago the first thing that struck everyone who saw it was the fact that the face seemed completely typical of many modern Jutlanders. Yet the body was over 2000 years old (see p 62).

This continuity of history possibly accounts for one of the Danes' most striking characteristics—their unity. Innumerable events highlighted this unity during the Germans' wartime occupation. When it became known, for instance, that all Jews were to be rounded up and sent to concentration camps the entire population buckled to and in a matter of days had smuggled every Jew willing to leave his home into Sweden.

Differences in social class and wealth are marked—but not resented. A managing director and his most junior employee happily sit side by side in a bar or restaurant with their respective girlfriends. Further, though modern Denmark is decidedly an urban nation, the ties between town and country are so strong that antagonism is non-existent. And for many years women have occupied an all-but-equal position with men.

Danes' and Britons' senses of humour correspond almost exactly.

In fact, the Danes' love of understatement and their refusal to get needlessly excited make British tendencies in this direction look amateurish. And their fundamental modesty shows up in many unexpected ways.

At different times Denmark has ruled the whole of Norway and Sweden, most of the territory bordering the Baltic Sea, and much of England. But no one in Denmark boasts about the country's imperial past nor mentions that the country is Europe's largest. Large numbers of highly successful Danish business men, including many millionaires, live in the village homes where they grew up.

Yet Denmark has innumerable astonishing achievements to boast about. The country possesses no sources of power or energy whatsoever. The only raw material found in its soil is china clay. Yet half the entire world's merchant ships are powered by Danish-built diesels. Danish refrigeration and air-conditioning plant, electronic equipment, drugs, and furniture are used throughout the world—to say nothing of toys like Lego, manufactured under licence in more than 50 countries: its inventor still lives in the tiny village where his contemporaries knew him as the struggling carpenter's son, making—at first—wooden toys to earn extra money.

Efficiency and success in Denmark are not considered to imply any degree of ruthlessness towards other human beings—quite the reverse. The Danes probably understand the importance of sound and satisfying human relationships better than any other nation in the world. Highly successful factory owners, for example, have been known to refuse to expand on the grounds that not being on Christian name terms with every single employee would reduce efficiency too greatly.

The office of Ombudsmand (Parliamentary Commissioner who deals with the public's complaints against state officials) has existed for a long time in the Scandinavian countries. The Danes, however, gave it a new and very modern form in 1953, making it possible for even the humblest citizen to approach the Ombudsmand in person, if he wished, without even making an appointment to see him, and giving the Ombudsmand powers to investigate virtually any matter he considered unsatisfactory and to make any recommendations he thought would improve public administration up to and including the impeachment of ministers.

When it comes to dealing with children, the Danes can teach the world a huge amount. All over Denmark you will find Junk Playgrounds, known for some reason in Britain as Adventure Playgrounds. They were invented by the Danes and the use made of them in Denmark goes beyond anything yet widely known in

Britain. Many, for instance, have facilities permitting children to keep pets that cannot be housed in normal flats and houses—Danish homes tend to have less space than is normal in Britain. Most Junk Playgrounds, too, are managed by committees of the children who use them.

It is not possible here to describe other imaginative schemes designed to help children. This little-known side of Danish life is worth investigating further.

On a different topic, many people who know Denmark only through lopsided, over-coloured, and often biased newspaper and television reports imagine it to be a hotbed of sexual promiscuity and unbridled pornography. Sex and porno shops do in fact operate with complete freedom and there is a corner of Copenhagen, in the Vesterbro quarter, where prostitutes of every type are openly available for hire. But if you stay any length of time in Denmark you soon discover that sex and everything connected with it is differently viewed from the way in which it is normally regarded in Britain and the rest of the 'developed' world. The Danes treat all this in a much more realistic way than we do. Sex for them is a fact of life, not something to be slurred over in public and sniggered at in private. It is accepted as something that people, and especially young people, are bound to be interested in. Children, whether born in or out of wedlock, are treated as completely normal phenomena. Having an illegitimate baby does not involve any sort of stigma for the mother.

But the Danes of course are not completely perfect. Some may strike you, when you get to know them well, as being a bit smug and complacent. Modern prosperity and full employment has had the effect in some places of reducing the standards of service that you can expect. But these are only minor blemishes. They have certainly done nothing to spoil what for foreign visitors is probably the Danes' outstanding characteristic—their hospitality. Wherever you go you will receive a tremendously warm welcome, especially if you are British.

History

Archaeological finds show that about 4000 years ago a race of farming folk moved northward into Jutland and the Danish islands. During the Bronze Age, 1500—500 BC Denmark was at the crossroads of north-south and east-west trade and obviously prosperous. Prosperity returned during the Viking period when trade as well as war and plunder took the sailor-warrior-merchants to many distant lands. At the peak of Viking expansion the Danish King Canute the Great (1018-35: the Canute we remember in Britain) ruled an empire which extended from the southern provinces of Sweden to the west of England. England was lost soon after Canute's death but expansion occurred again in the 13th and 14th centuries. King Valdemar Sejr (1202-1241) ruled south Sweden, the whole south Baltic seaboard including Holstein and parts of Mecklenburg and Pomerania, and Estonia (not yet converted to Christianity) as well as Denmark. Though Estonia was lost, his daughter married Haakon VI of Norway, eventually succeeding to both thrones.

The Faroes, Iceland, and Greenland became Danish along with Norway. In 1389 Margrethe invaded and conquered Sweden too.

Sweden, never very strongly held by the Danes, was lost in 1658. Norway however was not detached from Denmark until after the Napoleonic wars (in which Denmark suffered severely at British hands—it was at the battle of Copenhagen that Nelson put his telescope to his blind eye to avoid seeing his commander-in-chief's signal to break off the engagement). Norway became part of Sweden in 1814. Iceland asserted her independence in 1946, but Greenland and the Faroes are still ruled from Denmark.

Serfdom was abolished in 1788, an event commemorated by an obelisk still standing in Copenhagen's Vesterbrogade opposite the Central Station. When the system of communal tillage ended most peasant farmers moved their homes to their outlying fields and gave the Danish landscape, dotted with isolated farms, its present characteristic appearance.

During the Napoleonic wars the British blockade, the destruction of the Danish fleet at the battle of Copenhagen, and the severe bombardment of Copenhagen in 1807 did serious damage. In 1813 Denmark was literally bankrupt. But that did not prevent the Danes from introducing universal elementary education in the following year.

It was another disaster—the loss of the South Jutland province of Schleswig-Holstein to the Prussians in 1864 after a short but expensive war, that proved the making of modern Denmark. In the 1860s the Folk High School movement, started in 1844, began to spread throughout the country providing a remarkable system of adult education that still flourishes today. In 1866 Denmark's first cooperative store opened at Thisted in Jutland—and began a movement which is still one of the corner-stones of efficient Danish farming. The Danish Heath Society was founded in the same year to ensure previously unknown productivity for the soil, and in that period, too, the country's sports clubs, which still do so much to ensure a healthy nation, began to be formed.

This was the beginning of Denmark's modern prosperity. Extensive industrialisation began soon afterwards, quickly gathered momentum, and is now advancing very rapidly indeed. The overwhelming bulk of the population lives and works in towns. Yet despite the continuous loss of farm workers and the deliberate discouragement of farm productivity because of marketing difficulties, farm production is still rising steadily.

During World War II the Danes found themselves forced to surrender to the invading Nazis. But the overwhelming bulk of the population remained strongly pro-Ally and quietly and determinedly, in true Danish manner, did all they could to obstruct the Nazis. In the postwar years the country's standard of living has risen higher than ever, though inflation has been a major problem. Denmark joined the Common Market at the same time as Britain.

The Arts

Architecture has flourished in Denmark for many centuries. Though the names of few practitioners will be known to ordinary Britons—with the possible exception of the modern architect-designer Arne Jacobsen—there is a huge amount worth seeing. It dates from Viking days right down to the present.

The story begins with the camp at Trelleborg on Zealand and other Viking remains. It continues with the many fine castles and manor houses scattered all over Denmark but particularly frequent in southern Funen, where moated Egeskov is the finest example of all. Denmark's extraordinary architect-king, Christian IV (1588-1648), left a considerable number of fine buildings to posterity, including Copenhagen's Stock Exchange.

In Aalborg, Aarhus, Roskilde, Ribe, and elsewhere you will find delightful cathedrals dating back to the Middle Ages. Attractive, colourful village churches can be found throughout the country: they include the one at Jelling beside which Denmark's first king is buried and seven defensive circular churches, four of them on the remote island of Bornholm. Timbered farmhouses and village dwellings, black and white or gaily coloured, are even more numerous. And to complete the story there is a remarkable assortment of modern buildings that are not only imaginative and unusual but also thoroughly attractive, enjoyable, and practical. A few are mentioned in the text. But if you want to make a serious study of modern Danish architecture you should ask the National Tourist Office for advice on where to go and what to see. The Danes have long specialised in organising 'study tours'.

The fine arts have similarly flourished in Denmark during recent centuries, though only the sculptor Bertel Thorvaldsen (1770-1844) has ever become world famous. Even without visiting the big art galleries you will see a huge amount of sculpture used to decorate buildings and public places—and much of it is decidedly good. In painting the best-known names include: Michael and Anna Ancher, C. W. Eckersberg, Julius Exner, P. S. Krøyer, Johannes Larsen, Vilhelm Landstrøm, Olaf Rude, and J. F. Willumsen. Among sculptors Jean Gaugin (son of the French Impressionist), Kai Nielsen, Vilhelm Bissen, Astrid Noack, and E. Utzon-Frank are well known.

In applied art Denmark occupies a very high position. Years ago Danish cabinet-makers teamed up with architects (all of whom are trained also as designers) to make Danish handmade furniture as good as any available anywhere in the world. As long ago as the 1930s Kay Bojesen started his experiments with cutlery design that resulted in the mass of stainless steel tableware now produced by hundreds of manufacturers. The famous silversmith Georg Jensen gave silverware new dimensions. The ceramic products of world-famous firms such as the Royal Copenhagen Porcelain Factory and Bing & Grøndal and of individual designers have put Denmark in a class apart.

In literature Hans Andersen is perhaps the only widely known name, though the scientist Piet Hein's English 'Grooks' (as he calls his amusing poems) are appreciated in many countries. But despite the smallness of their market—even today only about 6 million people read Danish—there have always been plenty of writers and poets. The best known, apart from Hans Andersen, are: Ludwig Holberg, Johannes V. Jensen (a Nobel Prize winner), Martin Andersen Nexø, Kai Munk (murdered by the Nazis), Karen Blixen (who wrote in English), Nis Petersen, Hans Kirk, Jacob Paludan, Soya, and Martin A. Hansen. All are available in English translation.

Music thrives in Denmark, with orchestras and numerous concerts not only in the main towns but in smaller places as well. Among Danish composers only Carl Nielsen is well known to British audiences. But the Royal Danish Ballet holds a unique position in its own world. Not only are its standards extremely high, it also possesses a repertory going back almost 200 years, enabling us to trace in one company the changes made since the great Taglioni revolutionised dancing in the early 19th century.

One other aspect of Denmark's music deserves mention—the little parish churches that you see dotted across the landscapes contain an inordinately large number of first-rate baroque organs. Special tours are occasionally organised for keen organists, both professional and amateur.

Sports

Swimming There are hundreds of beaches on Denmark's 7300 km (about 4500 miles) of coastline. Most are sandy, wide, and backed by dunes. The bathing season lasts from May to September.

On many beaches, especially along the wild West Jutland coast, the driving of cars is officially permitted—in fact there are speed limit signs on the beach at Fanø.

Nude bathing is possible at a number of beaches controlled by the Dansk Naturistunion (I. G. Smiths Allé 7B, DK-2650 Hvidovre). It is also officially permitted inside signposted areas at Blaabjerg and Rømø in Jutland; Bøtø on Falster; and Albuen on Lolland. It is widely, though unofficially practised, on popular beaches such as those at Løkken, Skagen, and Norre Vorupør in Jutland; Tisvilde north of Copenhagen; and in various parts of Bornholm. In fact, it is being increasingly practised almost everywhere. Theoretically you can be fined for bathing naked at places where this is not officially permitted: in practice you will not be bothered if you make certain that other people on the beach accept the idea of your being nude. It should perhaps be added that nude bathing is a very old Scandinavian tradition: the only difference is that in times past the sexes were segregated.

Certain simple safety precautions are advised when bathing from Danish beaches. On Jutland's west coast the North Sea breakers can be enormous and currents in some places dangerous. Get knowledgeable local advice before deciding where to bathe. Remember that if a rescue operation becomes necessary you have to pay for it—and it can be very expensive.

Water-skiing is possible at virtually all popular resorts except those on the west Jutland coast. Specially good spots include Svendborg, several places on Bornholm, Aarhus Bay and Ebeltoft, the Limfjord, and the Silkeborg Lakes.

Scuba diving and underwater fishing are little practised in these northern waters.

Sailing is extremely popular. Boats can be hired through local tourist offices or in advance through Danish Boat Charter (Strandvejen 327, DK-2930 Klampenborg) or Maritim Camping (Jyllinge, DK-4000 Roskilde). Proof of ability to handle a boat is required. Motor vessels can be hired in the same way as yachts.

With 600 harbours Denmark provides plenty of variety. The only snags are: (1) that in enclosed waters you have to keep a careful lookout for the numerous ferries not always able to give sailing vessels right of way, and (2) if you tow a trailer-vessel of your own to Denmark, enquire first about slipway facilities as they are still somewhat scarce. Visitors' boats are regarded as sports equipment and imported duty free.

Fishing is one of Denmark's highlights. Sea fishing can be practised both from boats and from the shore, with catches including flatfish, cod, sea trout, mackerel, and gar-pike. In freshwater lakes and rivers rainbow trout, brown trout, and sea trout can be taken and the coarse fishing is as good as anywhere in Europe. Non-Scandinavians require a simple permit to fish in the sea. This can be obtained with the help of local tourist offices or applied for in advance from the Fiskeriinspektøren, Borgergade 16, DK-1300 Copenhagen K. State your nationality and passport number, and enclose an international reply coupon. Freshwater fishing involves obtaining prior permission from the landowner or angling club who own the fishing rights. You may simply have to pay a fee, or you may be obliged to take out temporary club membership. Again, the local tourist office will help you.

Golf Over 30 courses are scattered round Denmark. In every main town and tourist resort you are bound to be within easy reach of at least one. Standards are high, though the colder Danish winters usually make it impossible for courses to be in good condition except during late spring, early summer, and autumn. Visitors are welcome at all clubs and green fees are reasonable. Take your own clubs.

Tennis Every town and resort of any size will almost certainly have either outdoor or indoor tennis courts—if not both—belonging to clubs which always welcome foreign visitors. A small fee is sometimes charged for temporary membership.

Riding Horseback holidays have become very popular in Denmark in recent years. Touring, trekking, and training courses are all available. One of the most popular tours follows the old Military Road built through the middle of Jutland over a century ago. It is organised by the Jutland Riding Institute, Post Box 55, DK-7100 Vejle. But there are plenty of riding centres elsewhere: the National Tourist Office can give you up-to-date addresses.

Canoes and kayaks Kayaking is popular in Denmark, whose many lakes are ideal for the sport. Canoe touring on the rivers Guden, Sus, Skjern, and Stor (Gudenaaen, Susaaen, etc in Danish) are a Jutland speciality. In each case you can make a trip of about 160 km (100 miles). Canoes can be hired for about 30-35 kr a day.

At night you either camp on the bank or stay in one of the many local inns. Information can be obtained from the tourist office at Silkeborg, Jutland's main canoe-touring centre, and elsewhere.

Walking and cycling Country lanes and footpaths crossing hills and heaths and woodland make walking extremely pleasant in many parts of Denmark. Cycling is equally attractive, since it is quite possible to spend a whole day awheel and see no more than half a dozen cars at most. Bikes can be hired in most towns and resorts for under 10 kr a day. Vejle, Viborg, and Aarhus tourist office provide excellent—and cheap—cycling tours specially suitable for families.

Spectator sports Apart from football, which is as popular in Denmark as everywhere else, the main spectator sport is trotting. There is a particularly popular course at Charlottenlund, just north of Copenhagen.

Nightlife and other entertainment

Nightspots of every sort flourish in Denmark. The choice is not quite so varied in main provincial towns and tourist resorts as in Copenhagen, but in these places there is always a fair selection. Hotel receptionists and tourist offices will bring you up to date with the latest 'in' spots.

Copenhagen and the other major towns have theatres which stage plays and opera. Concerts and Copenhagen's Royal Danish Ballet have already been mentioned. Cinemas are numerous in all main towns—over 50 in Copenhagen—and show many British and American films with the original soundtracks plus subtitles. Smoking is forbidden in all Danish cinemas, and it is usual to book tickets in advance. This can be done by telephone (let the number ring till someone answers—Danes have used an electronic queuing system for years) and English can be used. You do not tip theatre or cinema attendants.

Denmark possesses also a fair number of what for lack of a better English word must be called 'funfairs'. The most famous of course is Copenhagen's Tivoli, described in our 'What to See' section. Simpler pleasures than Tivoli provides can be enjoyed at Bakken just north of central Copenhagen. Tivoli is open from May 1st to September 16th, and Bakken from mid-April to August 31st. Other towns have entertainment parks inspired by Tivoli and Bakken, and if you visit any of these spots you will not only enjoy yourself—you will also find out a lot about the essential simplicity of the Danish character.

Circus flourishes from April to September at its permanent home in Copenhagen.

Danish museums deserve a little special attention. Apart from the big, 'official' collections of art and antiquities such as you expect in any civilised country, there are also innumerable local museums and tiny private collections on view to the public. It was a Dane who said that every self-respecting town and village expects to have at least one museum. Many of these are extremely informative and others, like Ærøskøbing's private *Bottle-Ship and Pipe Collection* (Flaskeskibs-og Pibe Samling), absorbing and very revealing of the collecting mania that most Danes seem to be born with. Not all private museums are small. Of five notable open-air museums—at Lyngby (near Copenhagen), Odense, Aarhus, Haderslev, and Hjerl Hede—the last is a completely private effort.

Food

Though different from British cooking, the food served in Danish restaurants is sufficiently similar to cause Britons no difficulty. Cooked dishes include mainly grills, roasts, stews, and so on, served with a considerable variety of fresh vegetables. Given the high quality of the meat and the freshness and variety of the fish available in Denmark it is hardly surprising that most visitors enjoy Danish meals tremendously.

A number of typically Danish dishes are available—a soup, for example, made largely with beer and brown bread; a bacon omelette served in the frying pan; crackly saddle of pork served with sweet red cabbage; fried eel; pickled pork with potatoes and kale; and a number of desserts that use pastries, lightly whipped cream, and fruit.

One particular delicacy—Bornholm smoked herring—should ideally be eaten the moment it comes out of the island smokery. Anyone who enjoys good food will rave over it. The flesh is so succulent and soft that you do not so much eat the herring as drink it.

Chefs and housewives love to display their inventiveness in the *smørrebrød* they prepare, and many open sandwiches are indeed delicious. When eating *smørrebrød* the Danes tend to start with fish and savouries, and then go on to meat and sweet things. But there is no hard and fast rule.

Breakfast in Denmark normally consists of a sizeable pot of tea or coffee, 3 or 4 types of roll or bread, served with butter, and usually also a Danish pastry. Things like cereals and bacon and egg are almost always available as extras. Lunch is served earlier than in most countries—12 noon is a normal time and many restaurants have it available from 11.00 on. When working many Danes eat just a few open sandwiches with a glass of milk for lunch. Dinner starts at 18.00 and in many restaurants goes on being served right up to midnight or later. At home the Danes usually eat early and have coffee with a cake or other snack later in the evening. Your first contact with the Danes at home may well be an invitation to this coffee session.

If possible, avoid taking full board in any but the cheapest hotels and inns. Meals served even in ordinary restaurants tend to be enormous: in good hotels they are even bigger, and it just is not possible to go on eating two of them every day for a week or fortnight.

Drink

The commonest drinks in Denmark are coffee, tea, and milk. Coffee is served very strong and is usually very good, though not cheap. However, you should be warned that Danish coffee has a distinctive flavour of its own which not everyone appreciates. If you ask simply for 'tea' you will be given an English-style pot with a jug of milk.

A tremendous variety of lager beers can be had in Denmark. The Tuborg and Carlsberg brews are already well known in Britain, but you will find a considerable number of other breweries' products very palatable as you travel round Denmark. Draught is available in a number of places, and if you are driving you can always ask for a 'light beer' *(lys øl)*, which tastes like beer but is alcohol-free.

Apart from their beers the Danes' most characteristic drink is called officially *akvavit* (from the latin Aqua Vitae—'water of life') or *snaps*. It is a pretty potent and very pleasant spirit which you swallow at least half a glass at a time. It tastes horrid if you sip it. Cold beer is normally drunk as a chaser between gulps of akvavit.

Something of a ritual usually accompanies the drinking of *snaps*. When your host raises his glass and says *skaal* you must do the same. You then usually clink glasses with everyone present, take a good gulp from your glass, and raise your eyes and your glass again to the others before returning your glass to the table.

Apart from *snaps* Denmark produces a speciality of its own, called *Solbær Rom* (Blackcurrant Rum). A sweet cherry brandy, made by the Heering distillery and called Cherry Heering is also very popular. Both Heering and CLOC manufacture a number of other liqueurs as well as their own whisky and gin. Imported spirits, like imported wines, are heavily taxed and therefore very expensive, particularly when drunk in bars. Despite that they are becoming increasingly popular.

Coca-Cola and other soft drinks can be bought in all restaurants and snack bars, as well as at kiosks in tourist spots.

Pronunciation Guide

Danish is at least as irregular as English: words of apparently similar spellings often are not pronounced alike and letters that are sounded in emphatic or careful speech disappear completely in ordinary conversation. (Unlike most languages, the faster the beginner talks in Danish the easier he will be understood.) Many vowels include glottal stops—as in the Cockney version *li**le bo**le* for 'little bottle'.

Vowels

a	between f*a*t and f*a*ther	
	as in French e	
æ	as in f*a*te	
e	as in f*e*d	—when short
	as in rath*e*r	—at end of word
	as in f*a*te (can replace *æ*)	—when long
i	as in s*i*n	—when short
	as in s*ee*n	—when long
u	as in b*u*ll	—when short
	as in b*oo*t	—when long
y	as French *u* or German *ü*	
ø	as German *ö* (roughly as in f*u*r)	

Diphthongs

aj,ej	as in f*i*re
av,ov	as in h*ow*
ev	as in st*ew*
oj, øj	as in l*oi*ter

Consonants

d	as in *d*og	—at start of word
	silent	—before s,t or after l,n,r
	as in *th*in	—after a vowel
g	as in *g*od at start of word or in *ng*	
	silent	—between two vowels, or finally after vowel
hj	as in *j*ug	
j	as in *y*acht	
v	as in *w*ater	
	as in *v*an	—at start of word or syll.
w	as in *v*an	

Alphabet

The Danish alphabet has 28 letters. Æ, Ø, and Å (in that order) follow Z, and Q is not used. AA is equivalent to Å.

Vocabulary

Everyday Expressions

Mr	*Hr*
Mrs	*Fru*
Miss	*Frøken*
Please	*Værs' god*
Thank You	*Tak*
Good Morning	*God morgen*
Good Afternoon	*Goddag*
Good Day	*Goddag*
Good Evening	*God aften*
Good Night	*Godnat*
Good-bye	*Farvel*
Yes	*Ja*
No	*Nej*
How do you do?	*Goddag?*
Very well, and you?	*Goddag?*
Excuse me	*Undskyld*
I am English	*Jeg er engelsk (britisk)*
Do you speak English?	*Taler De engelsk?*
I cannot speak Spanish	*Jeg taler ikke spansk*
I want . . .	*Jeg vil gerne have . . .*
Come in	*Kom ind*
That's all right	*Det er i orden*
You are most kind	*Det er venligt af Dem*
Never mind	*Det gør ikke noget*
Don't worry	*Det skal De ikke bekymre Dem om*
Am I disturbing you?	*Forstyrrer jeg?*
May I introduce . . .	*Må jeg præsentere . . .*
I don't mind	*Jeg har ikke noget imod . . .*
I don't think so	*Det tror jeg ikke*
I am very grateful to you	*Jeg er Dem meget taknemmelig*
What is this (that)?	*Hvad er dette (det)?*
Like this (that)	*Sådan her*
This (that) side	*Denne (den) side*
It is (was) wonderful	*Det er (var) dejligt*
Will this (that) do?	*Kan dette (den) bruges?*
I agree	*Jeg er enig* (I agree with you)
Help yourself	*Tag selv*
What is the time?	*Hvad er klokken?*

In difficulty

Can you help me?	*Kan De hjælpe mig?*
I am looking for . . .	*Jeg leder efter . . .*
Can you direct me to . . . ?	*Kan De vise mig vej til . . . ?*
I am lost	*Jeg er faret vild*
Where is the British Consulate?	*Hvor er det britiske konsulat?*
Speak slowly	*De bedes tale langsommere*
I am hungry (thirsty)	*Jeg er sulten (tørstig)*
I am busy (tired)	*Jeg har travlt. Jeg er træt*
I am sorry	*Jeg beklager* (I regret).
	Undskyld (Sorry)
What a pity!	*Det var en skam!*
What do you want?	*Hvad ønsker De?*
What do you mean?	*Hvad mener De?*
I do not know	*Det ved jeg ikke*
I do not understand	*Jeg forstår ikke*

I do not agree	Jeg er ikke enig med Dem		
I do not like it	Det kan jeg ikke lide		
I must go now	Jeg skal gå nu		
It is forbidden	Det er forbudt		
It is urgent	Det haster		
Hurry up!	Skynd Dem!		
Be careful	Vær forsigtig		
Look out!	Pas på!		
Be quiet	Vær stille (or: Ti stille—stop talking)		
Leave me alone	Jeg vil gerne være alene		
I shall call a policeman	Jeg henter en politibetjent		
Help!	Hjælp!		

after	efter	more	mere
against	imod	much	meget
agreed	enig	near	nær
all	alle	next	næste
almost	næsten	not	ikke
among	mellem	now	nu
before	før	on	på
behind	bag	outside	udenfor
below	under	over	over
beside	ved siden af	perhaps	måske
between	mellem	quick	hurtig(t)
cold	kold	right	højre
downstairs	nedenunder	slow	langsom, langsomt
elsewhere	et andet sted		
enough	nok	somebody	nogen
everybody	enhver	something	noget
everything	alt	that	den
everywhere	overalt	there	der
except	undtagen	these	disse
far	langt	this	denne, dette
for	for	those	de
here	her	through	gennem
hot	varm(t)	too	alt for
in	i, inde	towards	mod
in front of	foran	until	indtil
inside	indeni	upstairs	ovenpå
last	sidst, sidste	very	meget
left	venstre	welcome	velkomst
less	mindre	when	når
listen	hør	where	hvor
little	lille, små	why	hvorfor
look	se, kigge	without	uden
many	mange		

Accommodation

I have reserved a room (two rooms)	Jeg har bestilt et værelse (to værelser)
I wish to stay for . . .	Jeg vil gerne blive her i . . .
I do not want meals	Uden måltider
I shall not be here for lunch	Jeg er ikke her til frokost
May I take a packed lunch?	Kan jeg få en madpakke?
I want breakfast only	Jeg skal kun have morgenmad

I want a room with one bed (two beds, a double bed)	*Jeg vil gerne have et værelse med en seng (to senge, en dobbeltseng)*
I want a room with a private bathroom	*Jeg vil gerne have et værelse med bad*
I am on a diet	*Jeg er på diæt*
I cannot eat . . .	*Jeg kan ikke spise . . .*
What are your charges, including (excluding) meals?	*Hvad koster det med (uden) måltider?*
Are there fixed meal times for (breakfast, lunch, dinner)?	*Er der faste spisetider for (morgenmad, frokost, middag)?*
I should like something cheaper	*Jeg vil gerne have noget billigere*
Have you a room with a better view?	*Har De et værelse med en bedre udsigt?*
I want to leave early tomorrow	*Jeg skal rejse tidligt i morgen*
Wake me at . . .	*Jeg vil gerne vækkes klokken . . .*
Can I have my clothes pressed?	*Kan jeg få noget tøj presset?*
Can I have my shoes cleaned?	*Kan jeg få mine sko børstet?*
Can I drink the water from the tap?	*Er der drikkevand i denne hane?*
I want a hot bath	*Jeg vil gerne have et varmt bad*
Is there a plug for my electric razor?	*Er der el-stik til shaver?*
What is the voltage?	*Hvad er el-spændingen?*
I have some things to be washed	*Jeg har noget, der skal vaskes*
Will you get this mended?	*Jeg vil gerne have dette repareret?*
When will they be ready?	*Hvornår vil det være færdigt?*
When does the hotel close?	*Hvornår lukker hotellet?*
I shall be very late	*Jeg kommer sent hjem*
May I have a key?	*Må jeg få en nøgle?*
Is there a night porter?	*Er der en natportier?*
Forward my mail to this address	*Vil De videresende post til denne adresse*

armchair	*lænestol*	coat-hanger	*bøjle*
bath	*bad*	cook	*kok*
bathroom	*badeværelse*	curtain	*gardin*
bed	*seng*	dining-room	*spisestue, restaurant*
bedroom	*soveværelse*		
bedroom (single, double)	*værelse (enkelt, dobbelt)*	eiderdown	*dyne*
		floor (storey)	*etage*
(with twin beds)	*(med to senge)*	hotel	*hotel*
		hotel-keeper	*hotelejer*
(with a double bed)	*(med en dobbeltseng)*	hot-water bottle	*varmedunk*
		key	*nøgle*
bell	*klokke*	large	*stor, stort*
better	*bedre*	larger	*større*
bill	*regning*	lavatory	*toilet, wc*
blanket	*tæppe*	lift	*elevator*
blind	*blind*	manager	*direktør*
boarding-house	*pension*	mattress	*madrasse*
board (full)	*fuld pension*	office	*kontor*
board (half)	*halvpension*	pillow	*pude*
bolster	*skråpude*	plug (electric)	*stikprop*
bulb (electric light)	*pære*	porter	*hotelkarl*
		proprietor	*ejer*
chair	*stol*	quiet	*rolig, roligt*
chambermaid	*stuepige*	quieter	*roligere*

radiator	*radiator*
reading-lamp	*læselampe*
sheet	*lagen*
shower	*brusebad*
shutter	*skodde*
sitting-room	*opholdsstue*
small	*lille*
smaller	*mindre*
soap	*sæbe*

staircase	*trappe*
switch (light)	*kontakt (lys)*
table	*bord*
terrace	*terrasse*
towel	*håndklæde*
wardrobe	*klædeskab*
washbasin	*håndvask*
window	*vindue*

Beach and Bathing

Where is the beach?	*Hvor er badestranden?*
Where can I bathe?	*Hvor kan man bade?*
Is it safe to swim here?	*Er det sikkert at bade her?*
Is it deep or shallow?	*Er der dybt eller lavt vand?*
Is the beach sandy or pebbly?	*Er stranden med sand eller sten?*
I want to hire a . . .	*Jeg vil gerne leje en . . .*
Where can I change?	*Hvor kan man klæde sig om?*
I cannot swim very well	*Jeg er ikke en god svømmer*
Help! Someone is drowning!	*Hjælp! Der er nogen der drukner!*
Can I go underwater swimming here?	*Er der undervandssvømning her?*
Bathing prohibited	*Badning forbudt*

air mattress	*luftmadras*
bathe, to	*at gå i vandet, svømme*
bathing cap	*badehætte*
bathing costume	*badedragt*
bathing hut	*badehus*
beach	*strand*
boat	*båd*
buoy	*bøje*
canoe	*kano*
cliff	*klint, skræt, brink*
coast	*kyst*
crab	*krabbe*
current	*strøm*
danger	*fare*
deckchair	*liggestol*
dive, to	*dykke, dukke, at*
fish, to	*at fiske*
fish	*fisk*
flippers	*svømmefod*
harpoon	*harpun*
jellyfish	*vandmand, vandmænd*

knife	*kniv*
lifebelt	*redningsbælte*
lighthouse	*fyrtårn*
mask	*maske, dække*
octopus	*blæksprutte*
pebble	*sten*
raft	*tømmerflåde, flåde*
rock	*klippe*
rowing boat	*robåd*
sand	*sand*
sea	*hav*
shark	*haj*
shell	*muslingeskal, konkylie*
snorkel	*schnorkel*
speargun	*spydkanon*
sun	*sol*
sunshade	*solskærm*
surf board	*planke til surfriding*
beach umbrella	*strandparasol*
tide	*tidevand*
towel	*håndklæde*

Camping

Where does this road lead?	*Hvor går denne vej hen?*
How far is it to . . .?	*Hvor langt er der til . . . ?*
What is the name of this place?	*Hvad hedder stedet her?*
Is there a Youth Hostel near here?	*Er der et vandrerhjem i nærheden?*
Can we cut across country?	*Kan man skyde genvej?*
We are lost	*Vi er faret vild*

We are looking for a camping site
May we light a fire?
Where is the toilet (washroom)?
I should like to hire a bicycle
Where can I buy methylated
 spirit (paraffin)?

Vi prøver at finde en campingplads
Må der tændes bål?
Hvor er toilettet (vaskerummet)
Jeg vil gerne leje en cykle
Hvor kan man købe denatureret
 sprit (petroleum)?

bottle opener	*flaskeåbner*	path	*sti*
bucket	*spand*	penknife	*lommekniv*
camp	*teltlejr*	river	*å, flod*
camping	*camping*	road	*vej*
equipment	*udstyr*	rope	*reb*
camping site	*campingplads*	rubbish	*affald*
candle	*stearinlys*	sandwich	*stykke*
caravan	*campingvogn*		*smørrebrød*
country	*land*	saucepan	*gryde*
field	*mark*	sleeping-bag	*sovepose*
ground-sheet	*teltunderlag*	store	*butik*
haversack	*skråtaske*	tent	*telt*
hitch-hike	*rejse på*	tent peg	*teltpløk*
	tommelfinger	thermos	*termoflaske*
hill	*bakke*	tin opener	*dåseåbner*
inn	*kro*	torch (electric)	*lommelygte*
lake	*sø*	waterproof	*vandtæt*
matches	*tændstikker*	wood	*træ*
mountain	*bjerg*		

Church

Where is a Roman Catholic
 church (Protestant church,
 synagogue, mosque)?
At what time are the services
 held?

Hvor er der en katolsk kirke
 (protestantisk kirke, synagoge,
 moske)?
Hvornår er der gudstjeneste?

Colours

black	*sort*	orange	*orange*
blue	*blå(t)*	pink	*lyserød(t)*
brown	*brun(t)*	purple	*purpur,*
cream	*flødefarvet*		*blåligrød(t)*
crimson	*højrød(t)*	red	*rød(t)*
fawn	*lysebrun(t)*	scarlet	*purpurrød(t)*
gold	*gylden(t)*	silver	*sølvgrå(t)*
green	*grøn(t)*	violet	*violet*
grey	*grå(t)*	white	*hvid(t)*
mauve	*grålilla,*	yellow	*gul(t)*
	lysviolet		

Days of the Week

Sunday	*søndag*	Thursday	*torsdag*
Monday	*mandag*	Friday	*fredag*
Tuesday	*tirsdag*	Saturday	*lørdag*
Wednesday	*onsdag*		

Months

January	*januar*	July	*juli*
February	*februar*	August	*august*
March	*marts*	September	*september*
April	*april*	October	*oktober*
May	*maj*	November	*november*
June	*juni*	December	*december*

Entertainment

Where is a good cheap night club? — *Hvor er der en god, billig natrestaurant?*
Would you care to dance? — *Må jeg danse med Dem?*
Where can I dance? — *Hvor kan man danse?*
What would you like to drink? — *Hvad ønsker De at drikke?*

band	*orkester*	night club	*natklub*
box	*kasse*	seat	*plads*
box office	*billetkontor*	stage	*scene*
casino	*spillekasino*	stall	*orkesterplads*
cinema	*biograf*	theatre	*teater*
interval	*pause*		

Food and Restaurants

Where is a good (cheap) restaurant? — *Hvor er der en god (billig) restaurant?*
Where is a quick-service restaurant? — *Hvor er der et cafeteria?*
Where is a good restaurant for sea-food? — *Hvor er der en god fiske-restaurant?*
Where is a good restaurant for local dishes? — *Hvor er der en restaurant med lokale specialiteter?*
Can we lunch here? — *Må vi få noget frokost?*
I should like a table near the window — *Jeg vil gerne have et bord ved vinduet*
I only want a snack — *Jeg skal bare have en hurtig ret*
I am in a hurry — *Jeg skal skynde mig*
I should like to wash my hands — *Jeg vil gerne vaske hænder*
Have you the menu? — *Har De et spisekort?*
I like it underdone (medium) (well done) — *Understegt (mellemstegt) (godt stegt)*
A little more — *Lidt mere*
That's too much — *Det er for meget*
I did not order this — *Det har jeg ikke bestilt*
Bring me another — *Må jeg få en andere*
This is cold — *Det er koldt*
I have had enough — *Jeg er mæt*
May I have the bill? — *Må jeg bede om regningen?*
Is the service included? — *Er betjening inkluderet?*
Is this correct? — *Er det rigtigt?*
Please check it — *Vil De regne efter*
I made a mistake — *Det var min fejl*
I'm sorry — *Undskyld*
Keep the change — *Behold byttepengene*
We enjoyed the meal — *Vi nød maden*

ashtray	*askebæger*	bill	*regning*
bar	*bar*	bottle	*flaske*

canned	på dåse	plate	tallerken
clean	ren(t)	saucer	underkop
cork	prop, kork	serviette, napkin	serviet
cup	kop	spoon	ske
dirty	snavset	tablecloth	dug
fork	gaffel	teapot	tekande
fresh	frisk	tip	drikkepenge
glass	glas	waiter	tjener
not fresh	ikke frisk	waiter (head)	overtjener
knife	kniv	waiter (wine)	vintjener
meal	måltid, ret	waitress	servitrice
menu, bill of fare	spisekort	water-jug	vandkande
not clean	ikke ren	wine list	vinkort

Food	mad, fødevarer		
apple	æble	kidney	nyre
apricot	abrikos	lamb	lam
artichoke	artiskok	lemon	citron
asparagus	asparges	lettuce	grøn salat
bacon	bacon	liver	lever
banana	banan	lobster	hummer
beans	bønner	marmalade	orangemarmalade
beef	oksekød	melon	melon
biscuit	kiks	mushroom	champignon
bread (white)	franskbrød	mussels	muslinger
bread (brown)	sigtebrød	mustard	sennep
butter	smør	oil	olie
cabbage	kål	olive oil	olivenolie
cake	kage	onion	løg
carrot	gulerod	orange	applesin
cauliflower	blomkål	oyster	østers
caviare	kaviar	pastry (cake)	wienerbrød
celery	selleri	peach	fersken
cheese	ost	peanuts	jordnødder
cherries	kirsebær	pear	pære
chicken	kylling	peas	ærter
chocolate	chokolade	pepper	peber
chops	koteletter	pickles	pickles
crab	krabbe	pineapple	ananas
crayfish	krebs	plum	blomme
cream	fløde	pork	flæskekød
cucumber	agurk	potato	kartoffel
dessert	dessert	prawn	stor reje
egg	æg	prunes	svesker
figs	figner	raisins	rosiner
fish	fisk	raspberry	hindbær
fruit	frugt	rice	ris
game	vildt	roll	rundstykke
garlic	hvidløg	salad	salat
grapefruit	grapefrugt	salmon	laks
ham	skinke	salt	salt
honey	honning	sardine	sardin
hors-d'oeuvres	forret	sauce	sovs
ice	is	sausage (beef)	pølse
ice-cream	is	sausage (pork)	pølse
jam	syltetøj	scampi	scampi

seafood	*fiskemad*	sugar	*sukker*
shrimp	*reje*	toast	*ristet brød*
snail	*snegl*	tomato	*tomat*
sole	*søtunge*	trout	*ørred*
soup	*suppe*	vanilla	*vanilje*
spinach	*spinat*	veal	*kalvekød*
steak	*bøfkød*	vegetables	*grøntsager*
strawberry	*jordbær*	vinegar	*eddike*

Drink

What would you like to drink?	*Hvad ønsker De at drikke?*
What would you suggest?	*Hvad vil De foreslå?*
I should like . . .	*Jeg vil gerne have . . .*
Your health!	*Skål!*
Just a little	*Kun lidt*
A little more	*Lidt mere*
That's enough	*Tak, det er nok*

alcoholic drink	*spiritus*	mineral water	*mineralvand*
another	*en til*	mug	*krus*
aperitif	*aperitif*	nip	*en lille*
beer	*øl*	orange	*appelsin*
bottle (half)	*flaske (halv)*	orangeade	*orangeade*
brandy	*cognac*	port	*portvin*
carafe	*karaffel*	rum	*rom*
champagne	*champagne*	sherry	*sherry*
cider	*æblevin*	small	*lille*
cocktail	*cocktail*	soda water	*soda*
double	*dobbelt*	spirits	*spiritus*
gin	*gin*	tonic water	*tonic*
glass	*glas*	vermouth	*vermouth*
ice	*is*	vodka	*vodka*
jug	*kande*	water	*vand*
lager	*pilsner*	whisky	*whisky*
large	*stor*	wine, dry	*vin, tør*
lemon	*citron*	wine, sweet	*vin, sød*
lemonade	*lemonade*	wine, red	*rødvin*
lime	*lime*	wine, rosé	*rose-vin*
chocolate	*chokolade*	wine, white	*hvidvin*
coffee (white)	*kaffe (med fløde)*	wine, local	
coffee (black)	*kaffe*	milk-shake	*milk-shake*
milk	*mælk*	tea (lemon)	*te (med citron)*
liqueur	*likør*	tea (milk)	*te (med mælk)*
non-alcoholic	*alkoholfri*		

Health

Send for a doctor	*Send bud efter lægen*
It is broken	*Er den (det) brækket*
Have you any bandages?	*Har De forbindingssager?*
Do not move him (her)	*Han (hun) må ikke flyttes*
I am not feeling well	*Jeg har det skidt*
I have a pain here	*Det gør ondt her*
I have a headache	*Jeg har hovedpine*
I have a sore throat	*Jeg er øm i halsen*
My stomach is upset	*Der er noget i vejen med maven*
I feel much better	*Jeg har det meget bedre*

Can you recommend a dentist?	*Kan De anbefale en tandlæge?*
I have a toothache	*Jeg har tandpine*
I want it out	*Den skal trækkes ud*
I should like an injection	*Jeg vil gerne have en indsprøjtning*
You are hurting me	*Det gør ondt*
Can you make up this prescription?	*Må jeg få en recept?*
When will it be ready?	*Hvornår er det færdigt?*
Can you give me a remedy for . . . ?	*Kan De give mig noget for . . . ?*
For external use only	*Kun til udvortes brug*
One teaspoonful (tablespoonful) in a glass of water	*En teskefuld (spiseskefuld) i et glas vand*

English	Danish	English	Danish
accident	*ulykke*	hospital	*sygehus*
ambulance	*ambulance*	illness	*sygdom*
bandage	*bandage*	indigestion	*mavebesvær*
bite	*bid*	injection	*indsprøjtning*
bleeding	*bløder*	insomnia	*søvnløshed*
blister	*vabel*	nausea	*kvalme*
boil	*byld*	nurse	*sygeplejerske*
burn (scald)	*skolde*	pain	*ondt*
cold	*kold(t)*	poison	*gift*
constipation	*konstipation*	remedy	*lægemiddel*
cough	*hoste*	sick, to feel	*at have kvalme*
cramp	*krampe*	sore throat	*øm hals*
cut	*sår*	sprain	*forstuvning*
dangerous	*farlig(t)*	sting	*stik*
dentist	*tandlæge*	stomach-ache	*mavepine*
diarrhoea	*diarré*	sunburn	*solbrændthed*
diet	*diæt*	sunstroke	*solstik*
doctor	*doktor*	surgery	*konsultation-sværelse*
faint	*besvimelse*		
fever	*feber*	swelling	*bullenskab*
filling (stopping)	*plombe*	temperature	*temperatur*
gas	*gas*	toothache	*tandpine*
hay-fever	*høfeber*	vomit	*opkast*
headache	*hovedpine*	wound	*sår*
Chemist	**Apoteker**		
aspirin	*aspirin*	prescription	*recept*
cotton wool	*vat*	quinine	*kinin*
gargle	*gurglemiddel*	sanitary towel	*hygiejnebind*
gauze	*gaze*	sleeping-pill	*sovepille*
iodine	*jod*	smelling-salts	*lugtesalt*
laxative	*afføringsmiddel*	sticking-plaster	*hæfteplaster*
medicine	*medicin*	toilet paper	*toiletpapir*
powder (talcum)	*pudder (talkum)*	vaseline	*vaseline*

Money/Banks

Where is the nearest bank?	*Hvor er den nærmeste bank?*
May I see the manager?	*Må jeg tale med direktoren?*
Will you cash this (traveller's) cheque?	*Jeg vil gerne veksle denne (rejse) check?*
What is the exchange rate for the pound sterling?	*Hvad er kursen på pund?*
How much is this worth?	*Hvad får jeg for dette?*
I should like some small change	*Jeg vil gerne have nogle småpenge*

bank	*bank*
cash, to	*veksle*
change	*byttepenge*
cheque	*check*
coin	*mønt*
exchange (rate)	*vekselkurs*
letter of credit	*rejseakkreditiv*
money	*penge*

money exchange bureau	*vekselkontor*
note	*pengeseddel*
pound sterling	*pund sterling*
rate	*kurs*
traveller's cheque	*rejsecheck*

Motoring

Do you know the road to . . . ?	*Kan De vise mig vej til . . . ?*
How far is it to . . . ?	*Hvor langt er der til . . .?*
I want some petrol (oil, water)	*Jeg vil gerne have benzin (olie, vand)*
I need . . . litres	*Jeg vil gerne have . . . liter (you mostly buy by amount of money)*
Have you distilled water for my battery?	*Har De destilleret vand til batteriet?*
Check the tyre pressures	*Vil De kontrollere dæktrykkene*
The pressure should be . . . in front and . . . at the back	*. . . i forhjulene og . . . i baghjulene*
I have had a breakdown (puncture)	*Jeg har motorstop (jeg er punkteret)*
Where can I find a mechanic?	*Hvor kan jeg få fat i en mekaniker?*
Do you do repairs?	*Kan De påtage Dem reparationen?*
I have broken . . .	*Min . . . er knækket*
This does not work	*Den (det) virker ikke*
Can you do it immediately?	*Kan det ordnes med det samme?*
How long must I wait?	*Hvor længe varer det?*
Where can I park?	*Hvor må jeg parkere?*
I want to hire a car	*Jeg vil gerne leje en vogn*
How much an hour (a day)?	*Hvor meget koster det i timen (per dag)?*
Is there an English-speaking driver?	*Er der en engelsktalende fører?*
Go more quickly	*Kør hurtigere*
Do not drive so fast	*De kører for hurtigt*
Wait here (over there)	*Vent her (derovre)*
Pick me up at . . .	*Jeg vil gerne hentes klokken . . .*
I must be back by . . .	*Jeg skal være tilbage klokken . . .*

back axle	*bagaksel*
boot	*bagagerum*
brake	*bremse*
breakdown	*motorstop*
breakdown truck	*kranvogn*
can	*dåse, dunk*
car	*bil, vogn*
caravan	*campingvogn*
clutch	*kobling*
convertible	*cabriolet*
cross-roads	*vejkryds*
danger	*fare*
distilled water	*destilleret vand*
drive, to	*køre, til*
driver	*fører*
driving licence	*kørekort*

exhaust	*udblæsning*
garage	*garage*
gear box	*gearkasse*
gear lever	*gearstang*
ignition key	*tændingsnøgle*
jack	*donkraft*
lever	*arm*
lights	*lygter*
lubrication	*smøring*
mechanic	*mekaniker*
motorway	*motorvej*
narrow road	*smal vej*
no entry	*indkørsel forbudt*
no parking	*parkering forbudt*
oil	*olie*
overtaking prohibited	*overhaling forbudt*

parking	*parkering*
pedestrian	*fodgænger*
pedestrian crossing	*fodgænger-overgang*
petrol	*benzin*
petrol pump	*benzinepumpe*
radiator	*køler*
repairs	*reparationer*
reverse	*bak*
road block	*vejspærring*
road junction	*vejknudepunkt*
roadworks	*vejarbejde*
roundabout	*rundkørsel*
school	*skole*
screw	*skrue*
screwdriver	*skruetrækker*
skid	*skride ud*

slippery surface	*glat vejbane*
slow down	*kør langsomt*
spanner	*skruenøgle*
speed	*hastighed*
speed limit	*hastighed-sbegrænsning*
steep hill	*stejl bakke*
steering wheel	*rat*
tank	*tank*
traffic lights	*trafiklys*
tyre	*dæk*
tyre (tubeless)	*dæk (slangeløst)*
two-stroke mixture	*totaktsblanding*
uneven road	*ujævn vej*
unscrew, to	*skrue ud, at*
wheel	*hjul*

Numbers

1	*en*
2	*to*
3	*tre*
4	*fire*
5	*fem*
6	*seks*
7	*syv*
8	*otte*
9	*ni*
10	*ti*
11	*elleve*
12	*tolv*
13	*tretten*
14	*fjorten*
15	*femten*
16	*seksten*
17	*sytten*

18	*atten*
19	*nitten*
20	*tyve*
21	*en-og-tyve*
22	*to-og-tyve*
30	*tredive*
31	*en-og-tredive*
32	*to-og-tredive*
40	*fyrre*
41	*en-og-fyrre*
50	*halvtreds*
60	*tres*
70	*halvfjerds*
80	*firs*
90	*halvfems*
100	*hundrede*

Photography

I want a black and white (colour) film for this camera	*Jeg vil gerne have en sort/hvid (farve) film til dette fotografiapparat*
Have you any fast film?	*Har De en hurtig film?*
Will you load my camera?	*Vil De sætte den i apparatet?*
Will you develop and print this film?	*Kan De fremkalde denne film og lave aftryk?*
I want one (two, three, etc) print(s) of each	*Jeg vil gerne have et (to, tre, osv) aftryk af hvert*
When will they be ready?	*Hvornår er de færdige?*
I must have them by . . .	*Jeg skulle gerne have Dem inden . . .*

camera	*kamera*
ciné camera	*filmkamera*
colour	*farve*
develop, to	*fremkalde, at*
enlargement	*forstørrelse*
exposure meter	*belysningsmåler*
film	*film*
film winder	*filmspole*

filter	*filter*
lens	*linse*
lens-hood	*modlysblænder*
negative	*negativ*
print	*aftryk*
range-finder	*afstandsmåler*
shutter	*lukker*
view-finder	*søger*

Post Office

Where is the nearest post office?	*Hvor er det nærmeste postkontor?*
Can I have a stamp for this letter?	*Må jeg bede om et frimærke til dette brev?*
I want to express this letter	*Jeg vil gerne have dette brev sendt som ekspres*
I want to register this letter	*Jeg vil gerne have dette brev sendt anbefalet*
I want to send this parcel	*Jeg vil gerne sende denne pakke*
Have you any letters poste restante for me?	*Er der poste restante breve til mig?*
I want to send a telegram to . . .	*Jeg vil gerne sende et telegram til . . .*
What is the charge per word?	*Hvad koster det per ord?*
I want a telephone call to England	*Jeg vil gerne ringe til England*
Will you get me this number?	*Kan De skaffe mig dette nummer?*
How much will it be?	*Hvad vil det koste?*
You gave me the wrong number	*Jeg fik forkert nummer*

call (telephone)	*telefonsamtale*
collection (of post)	*tømning*
directory	*telefonbog*
international money order	*international postanvisning*
letter	*brev*
letter-box	*postkasse*
parcel	*pakke*
postcard	*postkort*
post office	*postkontor*
postal order	*postanvisning*
postman	*postbud*
number	*nummer*
register, to	*anbefalet*
reply	*svar*
paid	*betalt*
stamp	*frimærke*
telegram	*telegram*
telephone	*telefon*

Public Notices

close, to	*lukke*
cross now	*gå*
engaged	*optaget*
gentlemen	*herrer*
information	*information*
knock	*banke*
ladies	*damer, kvinder*
no entry	*adgang forbudt*
no smoking	*tobaksrygning forbudt*
occupied	*optaget*
open	*åben*
pull	*træk*
push	*tryk*
ring (the bell)	*ring*
stop, to	*standse, at*
toilet	*toilet*
vacant	*fri*
wait	*vente*
way in	*indgang*
way out	*udgang*

Shopping

Where can I find a . . . ?	*Hvor kan jeg finde en (et) . . . ?*
How much is . . . ?	*Hvad koster . . . ?*
I want to buy . . .	*Jeg vil gerne købe . . .*
Have you anything cheaper?	*Har De noget billigere?*
I want more (less) than that	*Jeg skal have mere (mindre) end det*
I will buy this	*Jatak*
That's all	*Det er det hele*
It doesn't fit me	*Den (det) passer mig ikke*
It doesn't work	*Den (det) virker ikke*
Can you change it?	*Kan den (det) byttes?*
Will you change it later?	*Kan den (det) byttes senere?*
Can you refund my money?	*Kan man få pengene tilbage?*
My English size is . . .	*På engelsk er min størrelse . . .*

Will you measure me?	*Kan De måle mig?*
May I try this on?	*Må jeg prøve denne her?*
Can I order one (some)?	*Kan jeg bestille en (nogle)?*
Send it to this address	*Kan De sende den (det) til denne adresse?*
I will return later	*Jeg kommer igen senere*
It is too large (small)	*Den (det) er for stor (lille)*
How much each (per kilo, etc.)?	*Hvor meget koster den (det) per styk (per kilo)?*
Are these ripe (fresh)?	*Er de modne (friske)?*

Repairs

I have broken (torn) this	*Den (det) her er gået i stykker*
Can you repair it?	*Kan De reparere den (det)?*
When will it be ready?	*Hvornår er den (det) færdig?*
I have to leave by . . .	*Jeg skal rejse den . . .*

Hairdressing

I want a haircut	*Jeg vil gerne klippes*
I want my hair trimmed	*Jeg skal blot studses*
Don't cut it too short	*Ikke for kort*
I don't want any oil on my hair	*Ingen brilliantine i håret*
I want a shave	*Jeg vil gerne barberes*
Trim my moustache (beard)	*Mit overskæg (skæg) skal studses*
I want this style (show design)	*Som dette her*
I want a shampoo and set	*Jeg vil gerne have håret vasket og friseret*
I want a permanent wave	*Jeg vil gerne permanentkrølles*
I want a bleach (colour rinse) (tint)	*Jeg skal have håret bleget (farvet)*
I want a manicure (pedicure)	*Jeg vil gerne have manicure (pedicure)*
I want a face massage	*Jeg vil gerne have ansigtsmassage*
Thank You. That's very nice	*Tak, det er fint*
Could I make an appointment for . . . o'clock?	*Kan jeg få en aftale til klokken . . .?*

antiques	*antikviteter*	cheap	*billig*
bag	*pose*	cheaper	*billigere*
baker	*bager*	chemist	*apotek*
ballpoint	*kuglepen*	chiropodist	*fodplejer*
bathing suit	*badedragt*	cigar	*cigar*
bath salts	*badesalt*	cigarette lighter	*cigartænder*
battery	*batteri*	cleaner	*renseri*
belt	*bælte, rem*	clock	*ur*
better	*bedre*	clothes	*tøj*
blouse	*bluse*	coat	*frakke*
book	*bog*	coffee	*kaffe*
bookseller	*boghandler*	collar	*krave*
bracelet	*armbånd*	comb	*kam*
braces	*seler*	colour rinse	*toning*
brassiere	*brystholder, bh*	cotton	*bomuld*
brooch	*broche*	cosmetics	*kosmetik*
brush	*børste*	cushion	*pude*
butcher	*slagter*	cuff-links	*manchetknapper*
button	*knap*	cup	*kop*
camera	*kamera*	dark	*mørk*
cardigan	*cardigan*	darker	*mørkere*

delicatessen	*charcuteri*	longer	*længere*
department store	*stormagasin*	loose	*løs(t)*
		looser	*løsere*
dictionary	*ordbog*	low	*lav(t)*
disinfectant	*desinficerings-middel*	magazine	*blad*
		manicure	*manicure*
doll	*dukke*	map	*kort*
draper	*manufaktur-handler*	matches	*tændstikker*
		material	*stof*
dress	*kjole*	nail	*negl*
drycleaner	*kemisk renseri*	nail-brush	*neglebørste*
ear-rings	*øreringe*	nail-file	*neglefil*
elastic	*elastik*	narrow	*smal(t)*
envelope	*konvolut*	narrower	*smallere*
expensive	*dyr(t)*	necklace	*halsbånd*
fancy leather goods	*kunstlæder*	needle	*nål*
		newsagent	*aviskiosk*
face powder	*pudder*	newspaper	*avis*
fine	*fin(t)*	nightdress	*natkjole*
finer	*finere*	nylons	*nylonstrømper*
fishmonger	*fiskehandler*	pale	*bleg*
florist	*blomsterhandler*	pants (men's)	*underbukser*
fork	*gaffel*	panties	*dametrusser*
fur	*pels*	pen	*pen*
glasses	*glas*	pencil	*blyant*
gloves	*handsker*	perfume	*parfume*
gold	*guld*	photographer	*fotograf*
gramophone record	*grammofonplade*	pin (safety)	*sikkerhedsnål*
		pipe	*pipe*
greengrocer	*grønthandler*	plate	*tallerken*
grocer	*købmand*	powder	*pudder*
guide book	*turistfører*	powder compact	*pudderdåse*
handbag	*håndtaske*	powder puff	*pudderkvast*
hat	*hat*	purse	*pung*
heavy	*tung(t)*	pyjamas	*pyjamas*
heavier	*tungere*	radio	*radio*
heel	*hæl*	raincoat	*regnfrakke*
high	*høj(t)*	razor	*barbermaskine*
ink	*blæk*	razor blade	*barberblad*
invisible mending	*kunststopning*	refill	*refill*
		ribbon	*bånd*
ironmonger	*isenkræmmer*	rollers (hair)	*curlers*
jacket	*jakke*	sandals (rope-soled)	*sandaler (med rebsåler)*
jeweller	*juvelér*		
label	*mærke*	saucer	*underkop*
large	*stor(t)*	scarf	*halstørklæde*
larger	*større*	scissors	*saks*
laundry	*vaskeri*	shampoo	*shampoo*
leather	*læder*	shaving cream	*barbercreme*
light(er) (weight)	*let(tere)*	shaving soap	*barbersæbe*
		shawl	*sjal*
light(er) (colour)	*lys(ere)*	shirt	*skjorte*
		shoes	*sko*
lighter flint	*flintsten*	shoe-laces	*snorebånd*
lipstick	*læbestift*	shop	*butik*
long	*lang(t)*	shop assistant	*ekspedient*

short	*kort(t)*	sweater	*sweater*
shorter	*kortere*	sweets	*bolcher*
shorts	*shorts*	tailor	*skrædder*
silk	*silke*	tea	*te*
silver	*sølv*	tie	*slips*
size	*størrelse*	tin	*dåse*
skirt	*nederdel*	thick	*tyk(t)*
slip	*underkjole*	thicker	*tykkere*
slippers	*slippers*	thin	*tynd(t)*
small	*lille*	thread	*tråd*
smaller	*mindre*	tight	*stram(t)*
soap	*sæbe*	tighter	*strammere*
socks	*sokker*	tobacco	*tobak*
spectacles	*briller*	tobacconist	*tobakshandler*
spoon	*ske*	toothbrush	*tandbørste*
stationer	*papirhandler*	toothpaste	*tandpasta*
stockings	*strømper*	toy	*legetøj*
strap (watch)	*rem*	trousers	*bukser*
string	*snor*	umbrella	*paraply*
strong	*stærk(t)*	underwear	*undertøj*
stronger	*stærkere*	vacuum flask	*termoflaske*
suede	*ruskind*	wallet	*tegnebog*
suit	*sæt tøj*	watch	*ur*
suitcase	*kuffert*	wide	*bred(t)*
sun-lotion	*sol-lotion*	wider	*bredere*
sun-glasses	*solbriller*	wine	*vin*
suntan cream (oil)	*sol-creme (-olie)*	writing paper	*skrivebord*
		zip	*lynlås*

Sightseeing

What is there of interest to see?	*Havd er der at se af interesse?*
Is there a tourist information bureau here?	*Er der et turistkontor her?*
Is there an English-speaking guide?	*Er der en engelsktalende guide?*
I don't want a guide	*Jeg ønsker ingen guide*
I want to go to . . .	*Jeg vil gerne til . . .*
How much is this excursion?	*Hvad koster denne rundtur?*
Are there any boat trips?	*Er der ture med båd?*
How long does it take?	*Hvor længe varer det (den)?*
What time does the trip begin?	*Hvad tid begynder turen?*
When do I get back?	*Hvornår kommer man tilbage?*
We want to be together	*Vi vil gerne være sammen*
Can I go in?	*Må jeg gå indenfor?*
Is this the way to . . . ?	*Er dette vejen til . . . ?*
How far is it from here to . . . ?	*Hvor langt er der herfra til . . . ?*
How long will it take?	*Hvor længe varer det?*
I want a quick look round the town	*Jeg vil gerne have en hurtig tur rundt i byen*
Which way?	*Hvad vej?*
This (that) way	*Denne (den) vej*
I am lost	*Jeg er faret vild*
archaeology	*arkæologi*	cable-car	*kabine i tovbane*
battlement	*brystværn*	castle	*slot*
bridge	*bro*	cathedral	*domkirke*
building	*bygning*	church	*kirke*

city	*by*	monument	*monument*
coast	*kyst*	mountain	*bjerg*
excursion	*udflugt*	mountain	*bjergbane*
fountain	*springvand*	railway	
gallery (art)	*kunstgalleri*	pottery	*lertøj*
gallery	*kunstmuseum*	(product)	
(museum)		rest, to	*hvile, at*
garden	*have*	river	*flod*
gate	*port, indgang*	ruins	*ruiner*
gorge	*slugt, kløft*	seat	*plads*
guide	*fører*	square	*plads*
gulf	*havbugt* (if sea)	street	*gade*
interpreter	*tolk*	town hall	*rådhus*
lake	*sø*	valley	*dal*
law courts	*domhuset*	village	*landsby*
lighthouse	*fyrtårn*		

Sport

Do you play . . . ?	*Spiller De (du) . . . ?*
May I join you?	*Må jeg være med?*
Would you like to join in?	*Vil De (du) være med?*
Would you like a game of . . . ?	*Skal vi spille . . . ?*
Well played!	*Godt spillet!*
Where is the swimming-pool?	*Hvor er simming-poolen?*
Can I hire a bathing costume and/or towel?	*Kan man leje badetøj og/eller håndklæde?*
Where are the tennis courts?	*Hvor er tennisbanerne?*
Is there a golf course?	*Er der en golfbane?*
Where can I fish?	*Hvor kan man fiske?*
I would like to water-ski	*Jeg vil gerne stå på vandski*
How much does it cost for a tow?	*Hvor meget koster båden der trækker?*
Can I have a motor boat?	*Kan man leje en motorbåd?*
I should like to hire a sailing boat	*Jeg vil gerne leje en sejlbåd*
Can I launch a boat here?	*Kan man sætte en båd i vandet her?*
Where can I moor?	*Hvor kan man lægge til?*
Can I hire the necessary equipment?	*Kan man leje det nødvendige udstyr?*
Where can I go horse riding?	*Hvor kan man ride?*
Where (when) can I see horse racing?	*Hvor (hvornår) kan man komme til hestevæddeløb?*
Where can I find a guide?	*Hvor kan man finde en guide?*
What is the weather forecast?	*Hvad lyder vejrudsigten på?*
I am only a beginner	*Jeg er kun begynder*
Where (when) can I see a football match?	*Hvor (hvornår) kan man komme til fodboldkamp?*
What is the score?	*Hvad er stillingen?*

athletics	*atletik*	bait	*madding, agn*
billiards	*billiard*	fishing reel	*fiskehjul*
boxing	*boksning*	fishing rod	*fiskestang*
bowls (game)	*bowling*	float	*svømmer*
cycling	*cykling*	hook	*krog*
darts	*pilespil*	landing net	*landingsnet*
football	*fodbold*	line	*snøre*
Fishing	**fiskeri**	spool	*spole*

Golf	golf
ball	kugle
bunker	bunker
caddie	caddie
golf club (place)	golfklub
(driver)	golfkølle
golf course	golfbane
green	green
hole	hul
miniature golf	minigolf
putt	putt
Horse Racing	**Hestevæddeløb**
bet	'indsats
flat race	fladløb
grandstand	tribune
horse	hest
jockey	jockey
steeplechase	terrænridning
tote	totalisator
Horse Riding	**Ridning**
horse	hest
jump	spring
pony trekking	pony trekking
rein	tømme
ride	ride
saddle	sadel

stirrup	stigbøjle
Sailing	**Sejlsport**
anchor	anker
helm	ror
lifejacket	redningsvest
mast	mast
sails	sejl
Swimming	**Svømning**
bathing costume	badedragt
dive, to	dykke, at
swim, to	svømme, at
swimming-pool	svømmebassin
Tennis	**Tennis**
balls	bolde
doubles	double
partner	medspiller
racket	ketsjer
service	serve
singles	single
tennis court	tennisbane
Water Skiing	**Vandskisport**
motor boat	motorbåd
skis	ski
tow-rope	slæbetov
water ski, to	at stå på vandski

Tipping

Keep the change	Jeg skal ikke have tilbage
Tip	Drikkepenge

Travel

Train/Bus

Tog/bus

Can you help me with my luggage?	Kan De (du) hjælpe mig med min bagage?
I shall take this myself	Den (det) her tager jeg selv
Don't leave this	Husk den (det) der
Where is the . . . ?	Hvor er . . . ?
What is the fare to . . . ?	Hvad koster billetten til . . . ?
Give me a first- (second-) class ticket for . . .?	Jeg vil gerne have en første- (anden-) klasses billet til . . . ?
I want a sleeping berth	Jeg vil gerne have en sovevogns-plads
I want to reserve a seat	Jeg vil gerne have en pladsbillet
What time is the next (last) train for . . . ?	Hvornår kører næste (sidste) tog til . . . ?
From which platform (stop) does it leave?	Hvilken perron kører det fra?
Where is the booking (enquiry) office?	Hvor er billetkontoret (oplyskingskontoret)?
Do you stop at . . . ?	Standser De ved . . . ?
Must I change for . . . ?	Skal jeg skifte undervejs . . .?
Is this right for . . . ?	Er det det rigtige tog (den rigtige bus) til . . . ?
Where (when) are the meals served?	Hvor (hvornår) serveres der mad?
This seat is reserved	Denne plads er reserveret

Someone has taken my seat	*Der er nogen der har taget min plads*		
Can you find me another seat?	*Kan De finde mig en anden plads?*		
Is this seat vacant?	*Er denne plads optaget?*		
This seat is (not) vacant	*Denne plads er (ikke) optaget*		
May I open (close) the window?	*Må jeg åbne (lukke) vinduet?*		
Where is the toilet?	*Hvor er toilettet?*		
Where are we?	*Hvor er vi?*		
I want to put my luggage in the left-luggage office	*Jeg vil gerne stille min bagage i garderoben*		
How much do I owe you?	*Hvad koster det?*		
Taxi hire	**Taxa**		
Is there a taxi?	*Er der en taxa?*		
I am going to . . .	*Jeg skal til . . .*		
Here is the address	*Her er adressen*		
I am in a hurry	*Jeg har travlt*		
Will you drive as quickly as possible	*Vil De køre så hurtigt som muligt*		
Go more slowly	*Kør lidt langsommere*		

airline office	*luftfartskontor*	next (one)	*næste*
airport	*lufthavn*	next to	*ved siden af*
arrival	*ankomst*	number	*nummer*
bag	*taske*	passenger	*passager*
berth	*køje*	passport	*pas*
blanket	*tæppe*	pillow	*pude*
boat	*båd*	platform	*perron*
booking office	*billetkontor*	platform ticket	*perronbillet*
bus	*bus*	port	*havn* (harbour)
carriage (coach)	*vogn*	porter	*drager*
coach	*bus*	railway	*jernbane*
compartment	*kupe*	seat	*plads*
communication cord	*nødbremse*	seat reservation	*pladsbestilling*
connection	*forbindelse*	smoking compartment	*rygekupe*
Customs	*told*	station	*station*
Customs officer	*toldbetjent*	station master	*stationsforstander*
departure	*afgang*	stop	*stop*
dining-car	*spisevogn*	subway	*tunnel*
door	*dør*	suitcase	*kuffert*
driver	*fører*	taxi	*taxa*
entrance	*indgang*	ticket, single (return)	*enkeltbillet (returbillet)*
exit	*udgang*	tickets, book of	*billethæfte*
fare	*billetpris*	timetable	*fartplan*
half-fare	*halv pris*	train	*tog*
inquiry office	*oplysningskontor*	tram	*sporvogn*
journey	*rejse*	trunk	*stor kuffert*
label	*mærke*	waiting-room	*ventesal*
last (adj)	*sidst*	window	*vindue*
luggage	*bagage*		
luggage-van	*bagagevogn*		